STILL, I SHINE

REFUGEE TO RADIO, LIVING THE AMERICAN DREAM

Vildana Sunni Puric

Still, I Shine: Refugee to Radio, Living the American Dream

© 2018 Vildana Sunni Puric

Published by Lift Bridge Publishing
info@liftbridgepublishing.com
888.774.9917

www.lbpub.com

Contents

The Reminisce 1

The Childhood 5

Beginning Of War 16

Turanj Refugee Camp 22

Family? 28

Kupljensko Refugee Camp 38

Gasinci Refugee Camp 45

Welcome To America 52

The Early Struggle 60

The Man And The Grind 79

The Big Break 89

Detroit Radio 100

The Sunshine State 109

Big City, Not So Bright Lights 119

FOREWORD

The first time I saw Sunni, I was a freshman in community college. It was an evening panel discussion on working in radio. I remember Sunni's tight black ballerina bun sitting on top of her head and shiny black pointed-toe heels. She was smiling from ear to ear, and I later found out that she often does that while talking into the mic on-air.

"People can always *hear* your smile," she told me when I first started interning for her.

It wasn't until months after the panel, Sunni's name came up again. I was performing a poem for World AIDS Day and before my performance I introduced myself as a broadcast journalism major. The night before I had prayed for an internship and after my performance, I was spontaneously offered an internship at WPGC 95.5, the station Sunni works at. The woman who offered me the internship, Justine Love, was the director of community and public affairs at CBS Radio. She pulled me off stage afterward and told me she had the perfect person to put me with for my internship. Sunni.

I remember feeling my eyes light up -- Sunni was the only radio host I really knew of and I had just heard her speak months prior. It was meant to be, more than I even knew at the time.

The internship started a couple months later. On our first day, we were told we would rotate departments every few weeks. I was determined to stick with Sunni. I made sure of it. Every morning I would get her coffee (with two sugars) and come up with a list of story ideas for her show. It only took a few days for us to get really comfortable with each other and everyone around us could tell how close we were getting. I later found out she was Muslim too -- and I freaked out! No way! Our sisterhood was really meant to be. During the shift when I would have to complete a prayer (Muslims pray 5 times a day) -- she would lower the music down so I could pray in the studio. When people would ask about my hijab or if I drank, she would turn on big sister mode right away and get defensive and protective. On my 18th birthday she took me to a private dinner with Lisa Ling, a huge inspiration of mine. Whenever I shared my dream with her, of being a television journalist, she connected me with friends in the industry and talked about me to whoever she could. She would let me go on-air, write stories, and be her plus one at charity events. She took me under her wing and truly became my big sister.

I slowly learned her full story, the story you are about to read, and began to totally understand why she is who she is. She loves her job - but more so she loves to help and give back. She is the first to show up for charity and philanthropy efforts.

"If you're not poor enough to receive charity, you're rich enough to give it," she would always tell me.

I remember when she bought her dream car and finally became a homeowner how she would immediately reflect back to where she came from, and tears of gratitude would run down her face.

Sunni is open about her story -- she'll tell anyone where she came from and what she's gone through. But, what most people don't know is how true her strength is. I always joke saying if I ever was stranded on an island with one person, I would want it to be with her.

We've spent time in the jungle of Costa Rica together and I couldn't tell you anyone who is a more qualified "survivor" than her. Side note: She definitely used to audition for the show "Survivor" and I'm still waiting for her to make this happen.

Sunni is an inspiration to many. For her work, philanthropy, character, and the ray of light that simply emits even through a radio mic. She is one of those people who is genuinely happy to see the people she loves succeed and for me, she is one of the mentors that helped me see my own light. I guess why they call her, Sunni.

In this book, you'll meet Vildana. I didn't know that was Sunni's real name until months of knowing her well. It was for my first video story assignment in college, where I did a profile piece on her called, *From Refugee to Radio.* That was the first time I truly learned about her. We would google images of the Bosnian war and look for people she knew. She showed me some of the photos she still held onto -- and even though I've heard some of the stories you are about to read multiple times, I still ask her if this is all made up because it just sounds like a movie. There's no way this is real.

But it is -- and if you picked up this book because you love Sunni for the bubbly bundle of fun she is, you will finally learn why she is that person. Isn't that a beautiful thing? When you learn about why a person you love and admire is the way they are? It gives us incredible appreciation for the people around us and inspiration to connect with even more people.

I hope this story inspires you. I hope it shows you that absolutely anything is possible -- Sunni is a testament to that. Who would have thought a little Muslim girl in Bosnia would flee war and become the star she has become over American radio waves?

This is a story about life, triumph, perseverance, and finding the ray of Sunshyne at the end of what seems like an incredibly dark tunnel.

-Noor Tagouri, *Journalist*

THE REMINISCE

Sitting on the cool, shiny hardwood floor, I clutched a stack of papers like a trophy, in the other hand, I held a bottle of champagne, gifted by my realtor. Tears poured down my face. I could barely contain myself, "I am a homeowner!", I screamed inside my head. Every moment that happened before then was finally worth it. I had become a homeowner in Washington D.C., the most powerful city in the world, just a short distance from the White House – better yet the Obama White House! And I did it by myself, as a single woman, at thirty years old. I paused and wondered, "Is it really REAL?" Pinch. Yes. I couldn't move for an hour, just staring at the walls. Emotions overpowered me. I was finally "home". It had been a long time coming. I'd lived in many places and most of them never felt quite like home. The very thing I worked so hard for was finally MINE. The process of buying a house was grueling, from the paperwork to choosing the right place. All the stress, all the weight of the decision was on me. No husband, no kids, no family nearby … just a single thirty-year-old woman with a cat named Mason who was already scraping the freshly vacuumed carpet in the living room. No matter how I tried, I couldn't drown out the voice in the back of my head that kept asking me if I was truly happy.

"Is this what you reeeaally want? You worked your whole life to get here, was it worth it?" I felt like I'd promised them my firstborn in exchange for this small Columbia Heights condo in the nation's capital. The price tag was more than I ever imagined I would pay for a home, but damn, I finally felt like I belonged somewhere.

If you'd asked me years ago, I never would've guessed I would be here, a radio talk show host with a successful career, yet single and childless. Until now, I had always pictured myself married with kids by twenty-five years old, living on a farm somewhere in Virginia - you know, the typical white picket fence bullshit that you always hear someone talking about but never actually see in real life. At twenty-one, I thought that I would have all of that. At twenty-five, I said to myself "Eh, you got five more years". Yet, five years later, there I was. My number one goal had always been to be married with children. But as time went on and my career got going, I kept negotiating the ultimatum I gave myself. As Thanksgiving dinners passed one by one, my family grew tired of asking me, "Where is the man?", seeing that my answer remained the same: one day.

After a while, I made it a rule that no one, even my mother, was allowed to ask me about my personal life at the dinner table. In my twenties, I wanted a husband so much that even on first dates, I would picture how he'd look in wedding photos, how our children would look and if I could see myself being with him forever. I would try to figure out those things before I would even find out his birthday or what his favorite food was. If I found one little thing about him that didn't fit into my imaginary perfect life, I would get rid of him. Or he would sense my desperation and run, making everything fall apart. Over time, the dream of a white picket fence on a farm started to fade away. I needed to create an amazing life for myself even if I had to do it alone. I needed to find peace within myself even if the dream of the perfect family and marriage never happened. My mother and father met and got engaged within three weeks. They've been together ever since, but not everyone is that lucky, right? At times, I felt like finding the perfect man in this big ol' world is like finding a needle in the haystack. But there is no expiration date on finding love, right? I've learned that the best things will come when they are ready, if it's meant to be. Yet there was still an inner war within me, wanting that companionship I saw in my parents' marriage as I was growing up. Sure, all of those things sound so good and necessary to tell myself to feel good about my single self, but how much of that did I really believe?

Early in my radio career, I had a boss who was the most fabulous woman I had ever met. She was in her thirties, wore the hottest brand name clothing, had the most beautiful home, drove a Range Rover, and was extremely successful. But she was alone. No kids, no husband and her family lived all the way in Pennsylvania. She would entertain a few men here and there, but never anything too serious. So, even though I looked up to her in every way as an eighteen-year-old intern, was so fascinated by her lifestyle,

I would pray that one day I would be her- but not alone. I kept emphasizing the 'not alone' part making sure God heard my prayers and didn't skip over that small but very important request. Fast forward twelve years, and there I was with a carbon copy of her life. God must've not heard my prayers clearly because having a husband and kids were always at the top of my list. I had everything else, the career of my dreams, a luxury car, plenty of money, great friends, a social life… but no husband and no kids. So there I was, spending more money than I ever thought I would even have and investing into my future for the first time. Investing into ME, for me, by me, all alone. But as I sat there, I couldn't have been more proud of myself. It was a real feeling of accomplishment; I was sitting on top of the world. I felt untouchable. It had been a long and rough road. But finally, I was home.

THE CHILDHOOD

I can still see the glow of the sun, rising over the fields in my hometown village in Bosnia. We were young. We were innocent. My sister, my brother and I would spend hours outside, playing in the fields, climbing trees, gardening and swimming in the river behind our home. We lived in a small village in Bosnia called, "Dojnji Purici", and basically everyone who lived in that village was family. It was very common for Bosnian villages to be named after those who lived there. It was like a huge family reunion that never ended. Everyone built their own homes from the ground up and settled next to each other. We always helped each other whenever needed. My mother was a young stay-at-home mom, having all three of us before the age of twenty-five. My father was eight years older than her and managed our cousin's store a few homes over. He usually spent his twohour long lunch breaks at home, helping us with homework. My father was a quiet, reserved man. Growing up, one side-eyed look from him and you knew you were in trouble. He could punish you without saying a word. He was also extremely smart and one of few people I knew who went to college. Anything less than straight A's was never accepted in our house. We were always expected to excel at everything we did.

My mother, on the other hand, was a complete opposite, she was "my hot jalapeño pepper", as I called her.

She's 5'1 at best, small lady with so much spice. She was always very strict and the ultimate discipliner in our house. She had been with my father since she was 16 years old. She came from a small family from a neighboring village and her upbringing was completely different from my father's. My father had a huge family, seven brothers and sisters, all well-educated and established. Some of them lived across Europe and others in big Bosnian cities.

My mother on the other hand, came from a broken home. Her father divorced her mother, married another woman and had two sons and a daughter. Her mother moved away, married someone else and started her own family. So, my mother was left to be raised by her grandparents. That's one of the reasons why I believe my mother is so tough…she always had to fend for herself. Both of my mother's parents died early on and I never got a chance to really get to know them. My dad's mother Kada died right before I was born and my dad's father Ismet never remarried. He was the only grandparent I ever really knew.

My sister, Dina and I were eighteen months apart and we were inseparable growing up. She was a preemie baby and I was a 10-pounder, so despite our eighteen-month age difference, we looked like twins.

6

We dressed alike, had the same haircuts and did everything together. My brother, Aki was four years younger than me and you could always find him tagging along in our many crazy adventures. My sister was a lot like my father, just cool, calm and collected. I, on the other hand, was a burst of high energy. I always wanted to be the center of the attention and the life of the party and I always got in trouble for it. I wanted to be the first person to tell you the breaking news or any gossip going around the village, I'm pretty sure that's how I got my passion for broadcasting. I remember one year; my parents went away for a few hours. By the time, they had come back, I'd dug up the entire side of our house to plant my own tomato garden. They were furious. But that's the type of kid I was. Always getting into some type of trouble, with my siblings just a few steps behind me. The river behind our house was mostly uninhabited and my mother gave us strict rules on when and how we were to play by the river. During the rainy season, the river would overflow, always coming very close to flooding our home, bringing out all the garbage it had collected along the way. We were given strict warnings not to ever jump in the river since anything could've been at the bottom and we could get hurt. Clearly, I wasn't the type to listen, so, one day I jumped in. My friends cheered me on until OMG... I felt something digging into my foot. Once I got out of the river, I realized I had half of a broken glass bottle stuck on the bottom of my right foot. I didn't scream or cry, I was more terrified of what my mother might do to me, especially after she warned me to stay away from the river. I slowly tugged the glass out of my foot, limped back home, wrapped my foot with a kitchen rag and went to sleep.

It wasn't long before my mother found out what happened and followed the trail of blood back from the bathroom to my bedroom and found me sleeping with a bleeding foot hanging off the bed. Yes, I got punished - and that pain was worse than the pain in my foot!

We spent most of our summers with our old family friend Gzedo. She lived a few miles away from us, in a big house on top of a hill. She used to babysit us when we were little and we considered her to be like another grandmother to us.

My sister and I enjoyed spending time at her house. She had an older daughter who would come back from the city to spend the summers with us in the country. She would tell us fabulous city stories and dress us up in her 'grown up' clothes and makeup. Everything about the 'city life' was fascinating to us because we rarely left our village, only going as far as the neighboring towns. Gzedo and her husband owned lots of land and animals so helping them take care of the farm was the first job I had ever had. I was eight years old. Our main chore during the summer was to sweep the potato bugs off of the potato plant leaves and into a bucket to drown them in water. Have you ever seen a potato bug? Those things are HUGE! Not to mention, we did all of this in the scorching heat! Bosnian summers are known to get pretty hot. But Gzedo would always be sitting nearby in the shade with her many hijabs on and a cold glass of tea, cheering us on. For some reason she always wore three or four hijabs at a time yet, she was always cold, despite the weather being as hot as the Sahara Desert. I guess we enjoyed all of these outside chores because we never had them at our own house. Despite living in a village, we didn't own a lot of land or big animals, only a few chickens in the backyard. After we finished many of our other chores, like cleaning cow poop or helping her husband stack hay in the fields,we would be rewarded with the most delicious food. She would always make fresh mozzarella right in front of us and feed it to us with her bare hands right from the pot. I can still feel her rough hands pressing the fresh cheese into our little hands to make sure that we had enough. I learned later that during the time that we spent with her, she was really sick so those summers we spent helping her and her husband meant so much to them.

Eventually, we lost contact with them as we moved around during the war. Gzedo, like many other elderly, stayed back at home with her husband despite the turmoil. She eventually lost her sight at some point during that time that we had moved to America but would always ask the neighbors of how her little girls were doing... my sister and I. She died when I was a teenager and we never got to say our goodbyes. Her spirit was always so warm and pure, sometimes I still feel her presence around me. She taught me the true meaning of real hard work. I miss her. We weren't rich by any means, but we weren't poor by the standards of that time and place. We lived in a home that my father built for us, surrounded by huge hills and forests. We had a small old car and some land that was divided between my father and all of his siblings. We had no phone and one TV that we rarely watched because it only had two channels. Plus, we never liked being in the house. Only thing we enjoyed doing in the house was sleeping. To send us in the house especially on a nice day was the worst form of punishment for us. My childhood was rich in beautiful memories and adventures. I watched the sun rise and set every single day in awe. I prayed and went to the Mosque as much as I could. I felt spiritually connected to God and to everything around me. My imagination was out of this world. My family wasn't very religious, even though we were all born Muslims, but I was at that time. I enjoyed walking to the Mosque with the older ladies and wearing a hijab.

I studied the Quran and learned to read in Arabic. I was so proud of myself, it was a huge deal to me. I didn't know much or hadn't seen much outside of our village but I always knew the world was this big magical place I wanted to explore. I enjoyed reading a lot. My father always kept a huge collection of books and me and my sister would sit by the window and just read for hours every single day, especially in the winter. It was the best form of daydreaming. During the summers, we would swim in the river behind our house with the neighborhood kids and go fishing. On those warm summer nights, we would all lay on our balcony as my mother would sit nearby and slice apples for us. She would tell us the most amazing stories of her childhood, even scaring us with ghost stories she'd heard from her grandfather as we would gaze at the stars. It was something special we did with our mother often. Sometimes we would jump across the gates of a neighboring apple field and steal some apples for our nightly snacks since we didn't own an apple tree ourselves. There were plenty of apple trees there and I'm sure the neighbors never noticed.

On weekends, we would get up before sunrise to start our long walk to visit our step grandmother in the neighboring village. It was a few miles away through hills and forests, and despite my father owning a small car, we always walked there. The car was to be used for super long trips and hauls only. We didn't mind the three-hour walk too much. In fact, we would make pit stops along the way at friends' homes and they would always gift us with fruits and other snacks. In Bosnia, you could never walk by someone's house without getting invited in to eat and/or take home a gift, fruits, nuts and chocolates. So a short trip can turn into an all-day event. After my mother's father passed, her stepmother never remarried. She lived alone with our two uncles and our aunt, who was autistic. She was my sister's age but was very small and frail. She couldn't speak, only mumbling a few words we couldn't understand, but we loved spending time with her! Some of our favorite activities to do while visiting our step grandmother was to collect cherries from their many cherry trees and in the fall, we would collect chestnuts in their forest for the winter.

They lived in a two-story house that also served as a barn. The first floor housed the animals and the second floor was where the family lived. They had no plumbing or running water so when it came to using the bathroom, you had a small bucket and an outside stall. That was it. Whenever I would walk on the second floor, I felt like it was all going to tip over. But none of that mattered to us, we loved our family and truly enjoyed spending time with them. We were taught early on that material things didn't ever matter. It was all about the experiences, real love, and appreciating the environment around us, especially when we depended so much on the land to survive. No one cared about whose house was bigger or who had the better car. It didn't matter whether you had a car or not! It was always about family and community. Everyone always looked out for each other and would never let their neighbor suffer. That's when I learned the true meaning of happiness. I have been trying to get back to that point ever since. You know, that place where the simplest things matter the most, where you're completely free from the world's rules and standards. That simple country life was so beautiful, even a ray of sunshine on my face, felt like heaven. That place I still treasure in my memory. That was my childhood in a nutshell. The simplistic beauty that surrounded me, in nature and in our people, was what made me the person I am today.

In the early 1990s there were talks of a war and the village rang with gossip. As children, we weren't allowed into the 'adult conversation', but we knew that something was brewing. You'd catch the village men standing around on the corner smoking cigarettes, discussing the breaking news and the army. Women would be on the other side gossiping too, trying to keep it hush hush from us. But I wanted in, I wanted to know what was going on.

One Spring morning as we were playing outside in the little bit of snow that was left over from the Winter, a couple of war planes flew above the hills that towered our little village. As days started to pass, more planes were flying over each day. It started happening more often. I still remember standing outside of our home as the warm breeze brought in the fresh smell of newly bloomed flowers. I was watching the sky, waiting for them to fly over us again. It wasn't long before we started seeing the war stories on the news. It wasn't happening to us, yet, but it was happening close by. It was the fall of Yugoslavia. As a ten-year-old child, I didn't understand why the war was happening, I did understand that we were going to be affected in some way. In Bosnia, every man is required to go into the army once he turns eighteen years old. It's a requirement and an honor. So, I was mostly scared for my father because I knew that he and other men would have to leave us and go to war. If for some reason a man is not accepted into the army, he was looked down upon. Like there's something wrong with him and the neighborhood would gossip about reasons why he wasn't accepted. He would be labeled as an outcast and even for women, he wouldn't be the first choice as a husband.

The reason for the war and all the turmoil was never quite clear to us as children and the adults never discussed the news with us. But we started noticing that things were slowly changing. Trucks and tanks filled with military soldiers and heavy artilleries would drive past our house every single day. The small paved road where we lived was also the lifeline between Bihac and Velika Kladusa, two major cities in Bosnia. We saw all the action. We soon started seeing the UN trucks drive by with foreigners speaking English and other languages. We were fascinated. We've never seen people that looked different than us or spoke another language. I'm not sure who taught us that "gummy" meant candy, but as soon as we would spot the trucks rolling by, we would follow them up the road and yell *"Gummy! Gummy!"* The foreign soldiers would then throw whatever candy or goodies they had onto the grass, where we would scramble around, scraping the grass making sure we didn't miss any pieces. We started looking forward to seeing them every day. We'd line the streets with our hands up waiting for them to throw us those snacks.

Over time our basic supplies started to run out. It became more and more difficult to buy oil, sugar, salt, and other necessities. Then, we started living fully from the crops that grew around us. My mother cooked all the time, but it became harder to do as we ran low on basic things like salt and yeast to make bread. One day, we were playing outside, when suddenly, we heard screams and cries from our cousin's house across the village. Her young son was killed in a battle on the other side of Bosnia. The entire village gathered to comfort the family, as the children looked on. Soon after, her son was brought home to be buried. We weren't allowed to openly see his face or his body uncovered. Apparently, he was tortured. It was my first time seeing a dead body in front of me. He was beautifully wrapped in all white according to the Muslim tradition, completely covered. I looked on, watching my family members, completely heart broken and inconsolable. For some reason I wasn't afraid, nor did I cry. I thought to myself that he was probably in a much better place. Somehow even being so young, I sensed that things were going to get much worse. He made his transition to the other side, just in time. I was always taught to only fear God and nothing else.

Death didn't scare me. It was weird that I felt that way because when I first started going to the Mosque and learned about death, I spent those next few weeks crying every single night, praying to God to let my family live forever. Silly child. But now that the news reports started getting worse and we started hearing more and more men being killed, it didn't scare me anymore. It was as if my intuition kicked in saying, "You'd better toughen up now, because this is only the beginning." From then on, I've rarely cried when someone passed. Even at such an early age, I learned to build a wall to protect my feelings and my heart.

BEGINNING OF WAR

It was the summer of 1994 and our lives were very different from even the previous year. The war had taken a shift. Now the turmoil was brewing amongst our own people, Bosnians against Bosnians. Neighbors vs Neighbors. A civil war was under way and things were getting ugly. We didn't play outside anymore like we use to. There wasn't much laughter or happiness anywhere in sight. Our village was different, empty, sort of like the towns you see in all the zombie movies. The men would leave for days and weeks at a time, leaving women and children behind to take care of themselves. My dad was one of those men. His time away started to become longer and longer. We always kept our clothes and essentials packed in bags at all times, just in case something happened, and we needed to flee. Our entire household slept in one room, wayyyyyy in the back of the house just in case an attack happened. We wanted everyone to be accounted for, so we had to stay together. This was our reality now and we had to adjust and accept it.

My aunt and cousins came from a neighboring town to live with us because they weren't safe in their home anymore. With so many people from neighboring villages crammed into ours, our food supply started getting scarce. There were no more lamb and Italian bread dinners, no more delicious homemade cookies, or even juice. We had to salvage whatever food we had left and make it last as long as we could, because we didn't know when and if things would get back to normal. At the one and only grocery story in our village, bread and some basic necessities were delivered once a week. This was our only time to stock up. But because we had so many people in the village now from neighboring towns, we knew that these delivers were not enough. We needed more food to feed all these people. Waking up at 3a.m. to get in line at the grocery store became the norm for us. We would line up the streets with cardboard paper and blankets and sleep in lines, waiting for the food trucks to start arriving. It also became a social gathering for most. In line is where everyone would catch up on the latest news and local village gossip. With no other ways to communicate with people, this was it. But we knew that if we didn't get our supplies on that particular day, we'd have to wait until the following week. Eventually the store clerks had to put a limit on how many things people were allowed to get from the store in order to make the supplies last a bit longer and give everyone a chance to stock up a bit.

On an early June morning of 1994, we all woke up to the sound of loud chatter. It was a brisk morning with fog still settling over our garden, as the sun peeked between the two hills that were towering over our village. We rushed outside to see what was happening and saw a huge crowd, mostly women and children, all fleeing from the villages nearby. They were carrying bags and blankets, just like the ones that we had packed months ago. It was an organized chaos. Everyone was walking fast in a straight line, chatting amongst themselves, trying to calm the children who were dazed and confused. Many just waking up and cranky. It felt as if we all knew this day was coming so we weren't shocked … just sad and scared for what's to come.

My mother looked over at us telling us to grab our already-packed bags and hurry outside. As we collected our things, we heard machine guns and bombs going off in the distance. As the sound got closer, the crowds started walking faster and the real panic started to kick in. As a child, it felt like a movie. I couldn't fully grasp the seriousness of the situation. We ran outside - my sister and I squeezing hands, as my mother held our young brother over one shoulder and a big bag over the other. I started thinking about our dad, where he was and how will he know where we went? But we joined the crowd, quickly speeding up so we could catch up with our cousins who were a few feet ahead of us. The road by our house had a sharp right turn around the hill.

And as we reached that corner, I looked back through the crowd at my home somehow knowing this would be the last time that I would see it. All those beautiful memories and childhood experiences started to flash before I was quickly awakened from my daydream by the sound of gun shots that were really close. Pure chaos ensued as everyone was running for their lives hoping to find shelter just behind that sharp hill corner. As we ran, we spotted our grandfather in his car waiting for us on the side of the road. He had a very small car, the size of a Fiat, so I have no idea how we fit nine people in it, but we did. We sped away through the crowd of pure chaos, knowing that we'll probably never return and that things will never be the same.

We fled to our uncle's home in Velika Kladusa, which is a major city in Bosnia that borders Croatia. We always felt like outsiders in this big town because we were from the village. Most people in the city looked down on those from the villages because we spoke with a different dialect, dressed and moved differently. They would even call us names like "Seljaci" which was like saying "Hillbillies". It was the typical city versus country folk scenario. Classism at it best. My uncle had a big beautiful house that sat on top of a hill overlooking the city, surrounded by other beautiful homes. Mini mansions. At the time, there were around fifteen of us living in the house. We were pretty crammed, but we figured, it was temporary so we'd just tough it out for now. All the men in the family had gone to fight in the war, so it was just women and children and our grandfather. One hot summer day, around mid-afternoon, the warning sirens started blasting - which was unusual since we weren't close to the battlefield. We couldn't figure out what was going on since we had no way of keeping up with the news. Our electricity had been off for some time now. As we ran outside, once again we saw crowds of women and children walking up the hill, heading for the border. I heard my mother's voice scream from the outside telling us to grab our bags and head for the car. We haven't even had a chance to unpack our bags since leaving our village. As my aunt prepared to start the car, two men with machine guns and ammunition strapped to their bodies approached our house. They had camouflage uniform on with no clear signs or flags, so we couldn't tell which army they belonged to. They demanded that my aunt hand them the keys to the car. She looked at them with a stern face and said, "This is my car and you can't have it!" She knew that this was our only way to get the entire family across the border quickly and safely, so she refused to give up her keys. As my aunt got in the car, motioning for all of us to get in, the soldiers pushed her to the back of the car, got in the front seats and drove away.

They were headed straight towards the Croatian border and there was nothing stopping them. Everyone was too busy trying to make sure that their family is okay, to pay attention to anyone else. They didn't make it very far before running into a huge crowd of people, all trying to flee the country. My aunt sat quietly in the back seat, plotting her escape when she spotted police officers in the crowd. She pulled on the safety brake and screamed out of the window "Help me! These men kidnapped me! They're trying to rape me!" The crowd quickly gathered around the car preventing it from going any further and the men hopped out and disappearing into the crowd. All of this was unfolding while we nervously sat at home, not knowing if we should leave the country without her or not. The roads became even more crowded with folks trying to flee as the word spread that the other army was very close by and could start firing bombs at us at any moment. So, we patiently waited because we're a family and we weren't going to leave without her. To our surprise, we suddenly heard a car speeding down the dirt road... It was my aunt! She pulled up in front of the house, car screeching to a halt with dirt and dust flying all over everyone from her sudden braking. There was no time to rejoice in our reunion, after a quick embrace, we all piled up in her small car and headed for the Croatian border.

TURANJ Refugee Camp

We traveled for what seemed like a lifetime, stopping on the side of the road to sleep and to search for food and water. We ate whatever others were willing to share with us. We drank the water we found along the way from abandoned homes and wells. It was like an organized chaos. Miles and miles of women and children covering the road, many walking, some driving, and others on horse carriages. Some were dragging their huge bags filled with basically their entire livelihood, others were pulling a cow or a goat. The young, strong teenage boys were helping the elderly. Young girls were carrying the babies. At times it was silent. There was pain and fear on everyone's faces. We didn't know where we were going and who would be there when we arrived. What was going to happen to those who stayed behind? We were worried about our fathers and other men who were in the army. We didn't know if they were dead or alive, whether they were headed to meet us or if they were still fighting in Bosnia. With little answers and a few prayers, we kept moving. Until, we were stopped by the Croatian army.

Turanj was an abandoned Croatian town just a mile or so away from their big city, Karlovac. Turanj went through a horrific bombing the previous year and most of the homes there were destroyed. If they hadn't been leveled to the ground, they were so shot up by machine guns that most of the bullets were still visible all over the walls. The Croatian army told us we couldn't go any further because they didn't want Bosnian refugees mixing with the locals in Karlovac but we were allowed to stay put and set up camps. They warned us of land mines all over the city that were left behind from the previous battle.

The best way to stay safe was to stay on clear visible paved roads, drifting off into the tall grass meant there could be landmine traps there. Turanj had been abandoned for over a year so everything had been overgrown by weeds and high grass.

After a few days of sleeping on the street with thousands of strangers around, many people started to wander off to find shelter in the abandoned homes left behind. Hoping to find any clothing, food or animals left behind, many forgot about the soldiers' warnings about landmines and got hurt. This was our reality now.

My family was living and sleeping on the street. My aunt had parked her car on the side of the road and we put blankets next to it to "mark our territory". My mom and aunts would take turns sleeping in the car to help them with their back pains, but us kids didn't mind sleeping outside. We would huddle up and watch the stars, tell funny stories and eventually doze off to sleep. One morning as the sun came up and started beaming on our face, we realized that we were all covered in disgusting orange snails. Apparently, these little creatures loved warm bodies, so they came out in hundreds and covered all of us from head to toe. It was disgusting! Soon after, my dad and other men had left Bosnia and joined us in the refugee camp. It was great to have them back, we felt safe and protected again. The men immediately got to work.They used scraps and wood left behind of the destroyed homes and started building new small shacks which we turned into our homes. My people are so resourceful.

By this time, Red Cross and UNICEF heard about us and started to do food and clothing drop-offs at certain parts of the camp. There was no particular order in how things were received. We literally had to fight for the things we needed. I had always been the most social person in my family. So, I wasn't afraid to stand up to anyone, especially when it came to getting supplies for my family. I suppose I got my spiciness from my mother's side. On one cold October day, I overheard a group of women talking about a clothing drop and being the nosy mischievous kid I was, it didn't take long before I found out the location. During a clothing drop, the clothes would all be wrapped in a huge bundle weighing hundreds of pounds. Once the bundle breaks, it's every man for themselves. You may get one shoe and someone else gets another. If you can't come to an agreement of who keeps the shoes, then nobody will have them. I've always been a small athletic kid and once I arrived at the location where I knew the clothing drop was happening, I knew I would have to outsmart everyone. While women were fighting over scarves and tearing clothing from each other's hands, I dove under their legs and grabbed everything I could. I even had time to look at the sizes and put some things back I knew we couldn't fit or didn't like. It was safe to say that I didn't come back empty handed. Despite of my age, I still felt responsible for my family. I had a survival instinct, a drive, a special something that just clicked in my head and made me go for it. I was never afraid of anyone or anything. I was always more afraid for my family. How did they feel? Were they okay? I needed them to be okay - and as long as they were, then so was I.

My dad and uncles had patched up the side of a two-room building nearby. That was our official home. Our beds were made of wood, and oh, how I missed my mattress because sleeping on those wooden beds was worse than sleeping on the street. Our new home was right next to an army base that housed the Croatian soldiers. The base was there so the soldiers could keep an eye on us. A barbwire fence was the only thing separating our camp and the soldiers. Every day, we ate whatever was provided for us by the UN and Red Cross, mostly crackers, noodles, milk, and powdered potatoes. My mother had remixed all those things and came up with some delicious Bosnian versions that she cooked over a small brick oven that my dad had built in our "house". After a while, we got tired of eating the same things and we started noticing all the great foods that the soldiers had across the fence. You can smell the fresh Italian bread and delicious deli meats all the way into our little shack of a home. So, me and my friends decided the best way to get our hands on the foods is to actually speak to the soldiers and make friends with them. And that's exactly what we did. Over time, the soldiers would divide their food up to make sure we had a small plate as well. I'll never forget those acts of kindness despite our differences because they could've easily said no.

Despite our circumstances, we still found a way to bring some normalcy into our childhood. We didn't let our surroundings and the horrific things we witnessed break our innocent spirits. Our imagination still took us places as we played house in abandoned homes, shared the few dolls we had among us and dreamed of our futures. There was a huge river that ran along the road where we had set up our camps, so we spent lots of time there. Swimming during the warm days and sledding once the winter came and the river froze over. It wasn't easy for us to look over the bridge where we could see the skyline of Karlovac as we sat in complete darkness. We knew people there lived normal lives not even realizing how much struggle was happening just a mile across the river. I wished that were us. I wished we were going to school, watching television, and enjoying the simple things like we use to. I wondered if we would ever get back to "normal".

Winters in this part of the world are pretty harsh and living in the camp once the snow and cold came around became almost unbearable. Plus, we were told that the camp had to get cleared out soon.

They didn't give us an option to get transferred to a different place, we were basically told that we can either move back to Bosnia or get arrested. At this time, it was semi safe to return back to Velika Kladusa so we packed our things and started to figure out our way back home. Now that my dad was with us, we had accumulated a lot more stuff over the time that we'd spent in Turanj so we couldn't travel back in our aunt's car because we all simply couldn't fit. Day by day, the camp kept getting emptier and emptier. Walking around just didn't feel the same anymore, nothing but abandoned makeshift homes, dogs rummaging through empty pots and pans, garbage everywhere. It was time to go, but how? My father knew a man that had a tractor with a big trailer attached to the back. The man's family had already taken up a lot of space on the trailer, but he said if we can fit, we can ride back with them. And we did. The trailer had a cover on top, and supplies were stocked all the way to the rim … leaving little room for us to slide in and basically hold on for dear life during this ride.

But were just thankful for the offer because there was no other way that we would be able to get back.

FAMILY?

Once we arrived back to Velika Kladusa, everything felt different. The streets were empty and most of the homes had been ransacked by soldiers from the opposing army and looters. There were bullet holes sprayed across most homes, destroying the siding and roofs. My father and the other men were off to war again leaving the women and children behind to fend for themselves. My uncle's house was pretty big so naturally we assumed that we would all live there together again, the way we did before we left for Turanj. But things didn't quite happen that way. The neighborhood where my uncle lived was upper middle class by the standards of that time. Everyone was pretty well off there, even after coming back from the refugee camp. Having a roof over your head, garden, and some basic necessities stashed away meant that you were doing pretty well. My grandfather, who had stayed behind while we were at Turanj, was now living with all of us at our uncle's house. But after few days of him living there, we were told that my mother and us (the kids) had to leave and find a new place to live. I didn't understand why we were getting kicked out of our uncle's house, but at the time, there was no time to dwell on that, we didn't have anywhere to go!

We couldn't go back to our house since that part of the country wasn't safe, we had no money, no food and no resources. We were out on the street.

There we were, immigrants in our own country with nowhere to stay, not even with family. My father was away and there was no way to reach him. Even if we could, I'm pretty sure my mother wouldn't want to worry him about our situation, so she found us a place to live. It was with a woman she knew through family friends who lived directly next to my uncle's house. This house was lavish as well. The woman had three daughters and her own family members living there, so it was full to capacity. She couldn't offer us much, but she told us that we could stay in the empty attic, which didn't have electricity or running water. Despite her having running water in other parts of the house, we had to get our water from a well, that was half a mile away down a steep hill. We were just grateful that we had a roof over our heads. Our part of the attic was spacious though. It had a stove and a dining room table, but no beds or any other furniture. We did have a small balcony that overlooked the main street and we could see our uncle's house from there as well. Broken down cardboard boxes kept the concrete floor a bit warmer, and my mother laid several blankets over them to create our makeshift beds. We felt like we were back in the refugee camp, but this time around, we were the only ones. Everyone else was slowly getting back to their normal life. And there we were - the outsiders.

From that small balcony, we watched as other kids played outside, and led completely normal lives as we went hungry just a few feet away.

We didn't go over to visit anymore; it was as if there was an invisible wall between the homes and families. I started to be very worried about how all of this was affecting my mother. She was a young mom, in her early thirties at the time, and we could tell that our situation was becoming too much for her to bear. I'd never seen her like that, her spirit was broken. She's always been so strong, outspoken...confident. She was becoming a shell of her former self. Many nights, we would catch her crying in the bathroom, when she thought that we were asleep. She tried her best to hide her pain from us. We understood that everything we were going through wasn't her fault. We couldn't fully comfort her because our family has never been the "let's talk about our feelings and heal" type family. We've always been more of a "cry by yourself and work it out". It must've been a cultural thing because even when our loved ones suffered, it was normal to let them suffer in silence even if we knew what was happening. We were all about silent emotions, we knew that we loved each other and would do anything for one another-except sit down and really dig deep into our feelings and discuss the problems at hand. We were always in survival mode. No matter how tough times got, we didn't acknowledge the mental and emotional state as much as the actual events happening around us.

There was never time to be loveydovey with your mother, no matter how emotionally broken you or she were.

It was always "suck it up and keep it moving".

Every evening, we would gather around a small radio on the balcony and listen to the evening news, hoping to hear about our father. He had been gone for a while and we had no way of contacting him. We had no way of knowing whether he was dead or alive. Our hearts would jump every time they read the list of soldiers that died that day, praying that they didn't mention our father's name. Days turned into weeks, and weeks turned into months with no word on my father. Until one Spring morning, an injured soldier whose family lived down the street from us, came back home with a note from my dad. He wanted us to know that he was doing just fine, and he would return very soon. It was a huge sigh of relief for us. Especially for my mother, knowing that my father was alive gave her her spirit back... her light. Slowly but surely, she started getting back to her usual self. She wasn't spending the nights crying anymore and she was more loving towards us. All the energy in the house had shifted for the better.

Most of our meals consisted of boiled macaroni with a little bit of salt. We would also wet the spaghetti noodles, put them on a stove with some salt and pretend we were making pretzels. We had to get creative because that's all we had. One day, we got the word that there was a food distribution center for soldiers' families couple of hours away where we could go and get some basic necessities. We were pretty excited, but we had no transportation to the center. My mother packed up a small lunch bag and we started walking. What seems like forever and a day, it took us some time to finally arrive at the endless line of other desperate families waiting for food. All we needed was some flour, salt and oil. Maybe some sugar but that was a reach. At that time, that was a luxury. I hated drinking my milk without sugar, whenever we would have the luxury of scoring a cup of milk from somewhere. But when it was time for us to get our food, there was some type of misunderstanding with our documentation and we were told that we would not be receiving any supplies that day. My mother snapped, I had never seen her that angry. She got right into the faces of those soldiers guarding the doors, let's be clear that they were heavily armed with machine guns, and pleaded with them to give us something, anything. As tears ran down her face and her voice started breaking, I didn't care about being hungry any more. I wanted to protect my mother. I feared for her safety. They shoved us away and told us that there was nothing they can do for us. That moment will always stand in my memory because my mother showed us what real love and courage is. I knew that she was already broken so not being able to provide for us that day took her over the edge. She still had the courage to confront those men and stand up for her family. The result may have not been in our favor that day and we walked away without receiving food, but my view of my mother will never be the same. Standing at five feet tall, she was the strongest woman I had ever known.

The attic had a small bathroom that separated two halves of the space. There was an old man and his wife that lived on one side, and my family on the other. Since there was no running water in the attic, my sister and I walked to the well every day, sometimes a few times a day, to bring water for drinking, showering, toilet, etc. As young girls, we were so embarrassed because we were the only ones that had to do that in the entire neighborhood. We were already outcasts because we were poor village people trying to settle into the new city, but now we had to carry buckets of water up the hill every single day for everyone to see that we didn't belong there. My mother told us firmly that we were not allowed to go next door to our uncle's house and use their water hose.

Whenever I knew that my mother was preoccupied, I'd sneak into my uncle's backyard and fill up my buckets with water and wait twenty minutes before returning home. I wanted her to think that I had walked to the well. While I was in their backyard, I would steal their strawberries, but I'd have to eat them before I walked into the house because if my mother knew that I took them, an ass whooping would follow.

As time had passed, the area where we were living became dangerous again. Certain parts of the city were not safe because sniper shooters had taken over the hills above and were shooting down on civilians. Falling asleep to the sound of bomb explosions and machine guns in the distance was the new normal. I guess we'd grown so used to the rhythm of war, we learned how to tune out the noise completely. But that wasn't even the worst of our worries, we were still struggling. Our food supply was running low and we literally had no idea where our next meal was coming from. My mother's cousin who lived about 45 minutes walking distance away told us that she'd give us a bag of flour so that my mother can at least make us some bread. The only problem was figuring out a way to go pick it up. It meant that we'd have to walk through some dangerous parts of town to pick up this flour, but it had to be done and I volunteered to go get it. I guess my courage had taken over my fear because I wasn't afraid as I walked through the narrow streets alone carrying a bag of flour at 11 years old. I was more afraid that something would happen to the flour and that we wouldn't be able to make the bread that day.

After some time, we finally started adjusting to living in the city. We made new friends and even started going to school. Since the beginning of war, schooling for us had been sporadic and inconsistent. Whenever the government deemed that it was safe for children to start school, we would go but then it would be cancelled when it got dangerous. So, when we finally went, most of us got put in school according to our age, I was placed in the fifth grade, sometimes skipping grades and going to school mid-summer. I excelled at every single thing I did: my studies, sports and especially art. I always thought I'd probably end up being a painter or a fashion designer. Sketching different clothing designs and painting was one of my favorite past times. My sister and I made friends with these twin sisters that lived across the street from us. We were around the same age, so we made an instant connection, spending most of our free time together. One day, my mother walked in and told us to put on dresses and go over to the twins' house. I was confused because we never got dressed up to go across the street. We were usually in our shorts and dirty flip flops every single day. Then she told us that the twins' father had just been killed in the war and that they were bringing him home that day. We immediately ran to the balcony and could hear the screams coming from their house. The cries could be heard, bellowing down the street. It wasn't long before we saw a group of men, in army uniform, carrying a body wrapped in white sheets up the hill. We knew this was their dad. We all walked over and just stood outside as the soldiers put the body in the middle of their living room and the men went to the next room to pray. As people started to pour in to pay their respects, all of a sudden, a white dove flew through the front door, made a lap around the room and landed on the feet of their deceased father. Everyone just paused, we couldn't believe it. It got so silent that you could hear a pin drop. There's an old saying that as the soul leaves the body, it comes back as a dove to see its' family one more time. So, we believed it was their dad. The dove just sat there, not moving, just observing the people in the room as if it wanted to say something. As the prayers continued, the dove made another lap around the room and very calmly flew back out of the front door. That moment was always very special to me because I was very religious when I was young. For that dove to fly in during the prayer was somewhat significant to me. It showed me that God was still with us and watching over us…and that our situation wasn't permanent. But my views and my devotion to my religion changed shortly after that. I started saying that I was more spiritual rather than religious, despite being raised a Muslim. It all changed for me after seeing a devout Muslim man in our village pour concrete over a water well because he didn't want people to step on his grass. That hurt my heart because I couldn't believe that someone that studied Islam the same way that I did, could do that to his fellow man, especially during what was the hardest time of our lives. We had no running water at that time and as a kid, I was so hurt… I couldn't understand. It changed everything for me. From then on, I promised myself that I would work hard on being a good person. Not a good Muslim, a Christian, whoever … a good, kind hearted person to all. I told myself that if I never achieved anything great by society's standards, as long as people remembered me as kind … I would be okay with that.

It was a hot summer day, with a light breeze and the distant sound of bombs exploding. That sound had become the norm for us by this time, but today felt different. Somehow, I felt that today just wouldn't be an ordinary day. My anxiety was kicking in and my stomach was in knots. Even that morning felt different, the roosters weren't crowing, people weren't doing their morning walks and the streets were silent. Suddenly, the warning sirens started blaring all across the city. People started to pour out of their homes into the streets to find out what was going on. We knew the sirens meant that we were under attack…but what kind of an attack? We started seeing cars driving by fast, heading for the Croatian border on the other side of the hill behind us. We stopped one car to ask what was going on and an older lady told us that the city is about to be under seize and that everyone had to evacuate. We didn't ask any other questions, we ran back into the house and grabbed whatever we could. This time we didn't have our bags packed because we weren't expecting to flee again. We thought the next time we would move from this city; we would be moving back to our own house in our own village. My mother grabbed my little brother and a blanket. Me and my sister grabbed our jackets, shoes and a small bag of supplies. By the time we got outside, there was a huge crowd of women and children, all on foot, fleeing towards the border. Everyone was so caught off guard, so it was pure chaos. We joined the crowd and headed for the hills again.

Kupljensko Refugee Camp

It was déjà vu all over again. Women and children once again, carrying each other and a few things that they could grab just walking destination: unknown. Many were separated from their families, praying to find them in the large crowds. As we walked miles and miles, we rested along the way, checking in with people walking by us and asking if anyone had seen our father. With no telephone or other communication, this was all we could do. My mother looked worried. I could tell she was scared. We hadn't seen our father in a long time, we didn't know where he was or if he was even alive. As other fleeing soldiers started to reunite with their families, we just prayed our father was close behind. And he was.

Two days into our journey, we spotted him in a large crowd looking for us. It was one of the greatest days of our lives. But he was wounded. A bomb exploded near his post a while back and the debris struck him in the head. A small part of the bomb debris was still stuck in his head, so he wore a huge head wrap. But thankfully he was okay. As okay as he could be. To this day, the bomb fragment is still in his head. The doctors never wanted to remove it since it wasn't really bothering him. Removing it would have caused more damage.

As we journeyed across Croatia again, this time we didn't get very far. The Croatian army quickly stopped us and instructed us to set up camp along the streets and the abandoned homes along the way. This wasn't an abandoned city like Turanj, it was just a road in the middle of nowhere with a few homes that were far and few in between. Since this was our second refugee camp, we already knew what to do. Men got to work building small shacks, setting up tents and preparing for the upcoming cold months. We concluded that we would be there for a while and there was no way we were going back to Bosnia this time. We'd had enough. We wanted out. Anywhere but back home. The first week in this camp we stayed in an animal shed, sleeping right above the horses' stall. Well, that didn't quite work out for us because we all ended up getting lice from the hay that we were sleeping on. So, we got a tent from the Red Cross and my father set it up on the side of the road. There were a few houses that were across the road from us and everyone was scrounging to find shelter. It was first-come firstserve and we didn't get a chance to snag an actual room. But my father was so resourceful that he made our tent into a little house, he built an oven out of bricks and mud in the middle of it. It even had a chimney. As more soldiers made their way back and were reunited with their families, the camp started to look a lot like a real neighborhood. Red Cross had set up small clinics throughout, while UNICEF was doing weekly food and clothing distributions. There were a few water stations throughout the camp and everyone had to stand in lines few times a day to collect water for the family. This got really tough for us during the cold months. Especially when it came to washing clothing. It was one of the hardest things because in the Winter your fingers would literally turn blue and feel like they're about to fall off as you're scrubbing a pair of jeans outside in the snow. But everything became easier over time, we had to adjust. We'd been through this before, so we felt like we could do anything. The biggest thing I hated about the camps was the outside bathrooms. They were small stalls, made by the men in the neighborhood that were placed over a hole in the ground. The smell was terrible. At night we kept a "pee bucket" by us in case anyone had to go to the bathroom and in the morning, one of us would have to empty it. It was disgusting. Imagine having to use the bathroom right next to your family as they were sleeping. My dad and other men got together and created units within the camp, sort of like neighborhoods, that way it was easier to distribute food and clothing because they kept track of families, ages, sizes and other personal information. Bosnia's love for soccer ran deep so it wasn't hard to gather young boys around camp, set up teams, and organize soccer games. We kept ourselves busy!!! UNICEF opened women's tents where my mother and her friends would go and do "women things". I'm assuming that's where they got condoms, tampons, and other women hygiene products. There were a few hospital tents around the camp but those were only for emergencies. That winter, I got a bad toothache and the pain quickly became unbearable. I spent days laying in our tent crying, because

I was in so much pain and we had run out of medicine. One day as I was curled up in my blanket with my mouth throbbing from this unbearable pain, I asked my mother "do people in the world know that we're here and don't want to help us" ... I think about this moment a lot because there is so much pain and suffering going on in the world and the people going through it feel like they're invisible.

Finally, my dad had found a doctor that was willing to take my tooth out, but he didn't have any Novocain. At this point, I did not care because I couldn't take the pain anymore. I braced myself as I walked to the small tent at the end of the camp to see this doctor. All I remember was seeing the dentist utensils and a split second later, I felt like I had died. It was the worst, most painful experience of my life. It didn't help that I actually heard the cracking of the tooth as the dentist yanked it out of my mouth. No Novocain. Nothing. One of my worst childhood memories.

The winter was in full swing with no talks about us going anywhere so we had to make sure that we were prepared for what was coming. We expected lots of snow. My dad stocked up on wood and made sure that the small stove that he had built in the tent was still properly working. We collected extra boxes and blankets to line the inside of our tent to prevent the heat from going out. One morning after a big snowstorm, we woke up with our tent completely caved in on us. It couldn't handle the heavy snowfall. We had to move our family to a sturdier structure. We eventually found a small shack on a side of the hill that all five of us could fit into and we made that our new home. We never had pets growing up, outside of my dad's hunter dog, but some reason while we lived in that tent, we had a cat.

Well, we didn't have her, she had us. She would come around every day hoping to get some food that we had left over. After we packed our tent and moved into our new sturdier home, the cat kept coming around and would sit in the spot where our tent use to be. As we walked by, we'd glance over, and she'd just be sitting there waiting for us to return. It was pretty sad because we literally couldn't afford to take her with us, we couldn't be responsible for another living thing.

We had some cousins and friends that lived nearby our new place. We spent our winter playing cards, sledding, and just trying to make the best of what we had. Our time in the camp felt like it was standing still. Maybe because we didn't have much to do or anywhere to go so every day felt like a lifetime.

As Spring came around, there were talks of another camp in Croatia called Gasinci that was supposed to be really nice and that soon we would be allowed to relocate there. We heard that people there actually lived in trailers, had running water in the community center and were receiving cooked meals. Thus far our camps had been getting crackers in huge metal boxes that had to be pried open, and powdered orange juice. I assumed it was a cheap version of Tang because after drinking a cup, I had gotten really ill. It gave me the worst migraines and ever since then, I can't stand the smell of oranges, limes, anything citrus. Gasinci was the camp where we wanted to be, so we immediately applied and waited to hear on our status.

Outsiders weren't allowed to visit us in the camps, but there were a few exceptions. Once in a while, they would open the border and allow families from Europe to come in and bring food, clothing, money, to the people in the camps. We have an aunt that lives in Slovenia and we were excited to hear that she was trying to come visit us since we hadn't seen her in years. She also had two daughters that were a bit older than me and my sister, so we were hoping that she was bringing us some of their clothes. We made our way to the border of the camp, which was heavily guarded by the Croatian army, and anxiously waited for hours behind a barbwire fence hoping to see our aunt. She never came. We were disappointed because we really missed her. Also, we really needed some of the supplies that she was supposed to bring us. We later learned that she was at the border, but the army never allowed them to get near us. She had brought lots of bags filled with clothing and food, but she was forced to turn around and drive back to Slovenia.

The next day we were approved to go to our new camp, Gasinci. This being our third refugee camp, the idea that we really may never go back to our village started to settle in. I left a lot of my friends behind in Camp Kupljensko, but I figured their families would also get approved and follow us to the new camp. It didn't happen. Some families just got tired of waiting around and the struggle in the camp got to them so they decided to return back home to Bosnia. They felt that even if the situation back home is dangerous, they'll at least have their homes and they'll survive somehow. My mother kept reminding us that we were not going to go back home. Every day she would reiterate that there wasn't much for us back home and that even our childhood home in the village was ruined. We'd been through so much already and she wasn't going to let another ultimate goal, which was to eventually resettle somewhere in Europe. Some people were allowed to move with their families in Germany and Austria, but we had no families there. We decided we were going to wait it out, no matter how long it took.

GASINCI REFUGEE CAMP

When we arrived in the camp Gasinci, it was like a whole new world to us.

There were small trailers assigned to each family, community centers with REAL showers and Laundromats. I hadn't taken a shower in a real bathroom in over a year, especially with running warm water? We haven't had running water for so long that we forgot what it's like to take a shower with it. Usually we'd have to fetch enough water first, bring it home and boil it. Then mix the hot and cold water in a separate bucket to make enough lukewarm water for one person to shower with, grab a coffee mug or a cup, and take a shower... outside! Our makeshift bathrooms use to serve as showers as well. You'd use one hand to scoop the water from the bucket, and another hand to lather up. Rinse and repeat, all while the cold wind is blowing through a hollow makeshift bathroom outside. A real bathroom with real walls and showers sounded like heaven on earth at this time.

This camp even had a movie theater that would screen American movies once a week. The trailers were pretty small and five of us had to share it with another couple. There were seven of us sleeping in bunk beds all facing different ways with our clothing bags at our feet. We made it work somehow. We figured we had been through worse. All we did in the trailers was sleep because there wasn't any room left to do much else. But we didn't care, we were happy here. Anything beats living on the street.

The camp was very organized, and everything ran smoothly. Everyone knew their place. There was a huge center where the food was served 3 times a day, but you had to wait in long lines to get it. Each family was assigned a card to let the officials know how many family members you had and how much food you should receive. Every single day, we'd grab our family card and head for the line to get breakfast, lunch and dinner. Me and my siblings took turns to go get the food since we all hated waiting in lines. This camp was in a secluded area of Croatia and was built specifically for the refugees. There was nothing close by. No homes or any other residents. A bus program was set up through the camp officials, where a certain number of people per day would be allowed to leave the camp and go to the nearest city. We would have to get up pretty early and wait in line to get a pass to leave the camp and get on the bus. The bus was guarded by the Croatian army. They would take us into the city, let us hang out for a bit and then bring us back. My friends and I were eleven years old.

This was our way of getting out and seeing the world. We'd go into town and have ice cream and admire all the other teenagers walking by. We obviously weren't dressed in the latest fashions and we knew that those kids could tell we were refugees. We weren't really that embarrassed because we were just happy that we were safe. But we couldn't help to wonder when it was going to be our turn to finally be regular teenagers.

Most kids in the camp bonded over our similar struggles. We all had already been through one or two camps, many had their fathers killed, and we had all been very poor at some point in our lives. Our struggles connected us and brought us together. We never compared clothes or made fun of each other for anything because we were all the same. We didn't realize just how poor we were because everyone around us was the same way - poor. The camp also allowed men and women to leave the camp for a certain amount of days to go work on Croatian farms. Farm owners would come by the camp and pick up those who were willing to pick potatoes or corn for a few coins a day. My dad always jumped at the opportunity to go earn some money for the family. I knew it had to be hard for him as a college educated man to pick potatoes on a farm for pennies a day, but that's the kind of man he was… a great one. He wanted us to feel like normal teenagers, so he'd always give us some money to buy ice cream and teen magazines. That's how we discovered The Backstreet Boys and Spice Girls. Thanks Dad! Oh, and my best friend had a poster of Michael Jackson in her trailer. Now looking back, how the hell did she even know who Michael was and where did she find this poster? But it was there, King of Pop!

We were placed in a makeshift school as the camp officials tried to make our lives as normal as possible.

All the students were given a choice to study English or German, and most of us took up German thinking that we would probably end up in Germany. America had never even crossed our mind.

We were typical teenagers, reading teen magazines and gushing over boys. I had a lot of friends at the camp. My clique was about fifteen girls deep and we did everything together.

All the girls would gather in front of the community center and we would take our evening walks together. We'd play double Dutch in the street and discuss our plans for the future. We all had such big dreams and we knew that we couldn't live in these camps forever. We were always very optimistic for the future.

Most of us were involved in the folk-dance class that was organized by some of the older ladies in the camp. Whatever you were good at, that's what you contributed to the camp. If you use to be a dance teacher, then you started a dance class in the camp to keep the kids busy, etc. Everybody contributed to make sure we had somewhat of a normal experience as children. We even took a school field trip to the zoo and to a mountain lodge. For many of us, being from small villages across Bosnia, this was the most fascinating event of our lives. I had never been to a zoo or taken a ski lift to a mountain resort. It was just a day trip, but it was so amazing to us. In Gasinci, we were even allowed to have visitors. Our aunt from Slovenia was finally able to come visit, bringing us clothing and food. There was a mosque in the camp and I couldn't wait to go there to study my Quran. I started attending lectures every day and going in for the evening prayers. I genuinely loved wearing my hijab and being amongst all the older people at the mosque. It made me feel accomplished, I felt proud, never feeling like the refugee that I was. It was this beautiful feeling of being so connected to God. Most times I'd go to Mosque by myself, because most of my friends would be out playing, but I loved it that way. I knew that all the pain that we had went through was preparing us for something great, so I'd sit and talk to God myself.

One day, my parents told us that we had to get ready for a trip outside the camp for an interview. We were confused. What interview? It turns out that it was an interview with an agency that would send us out of the camp if we passed all the tests. Send us where? Where are we going? As kids, we didn't really understand what was happening. We were told to be on our best behavior and to wear decent clean clothes. We arrived by the bus in one of Croatia's biggest cities nearby. We pulled up in front of a huge building, the tallest one I had ever seen up close in my life. When we got in the building, we were told to wait in the long dark hallway. They called us into the interview room, one by one. They asked us all types of questions about the war and what we had seen. What we knew about our dad's army ties and things like that. We didn't know much. The details of the war were never discussed with children, so we were as honest as we could be. Sitting in the interview chair, my anxiety started to kick in. What if I answered

49

something wrong and ruined this chance for the whole family? I didn't know what the wrong or right answers were, so I was truthful. Whew! We passed the first interview, but there were two more. The entire process took a few months. We were always in the state of uncertainty because we desperately wanted to be relocated, but we didn't know if we fit the "criteria". One day, we received a letter letting us know that we had officially been accepted into the relocation program. By this time, many others in the camp were leaving as well. We always knew it was temporary so as soon as people arrived at the camp, they were already looking for a way out. People either got tired of waiting and went back to their homes in Bosnia or were sent to other countries to be reunited with family members. There were also other countries that opened their borders to refugees. People were being sent to these countries whether they had relatives there or not. I was happy we were finally going to go somewhere and start a new life with a real home, but I was sad to leave my friends. We all had created a bond in the camp and I didn't know what everyone's futures held. My uncle and his family had already moved to the United States, which is one of the reasons that we were approved. He had signed off on our papers. Refugees were more likely to succeed if they had family in the area, so having my uncle there let officials know that we were all going to stick together.

It was a cold, snowy, January morning and we were all packed and ready to go to America. The year was 1997. We met up with our friends at the camp's entrance to say our goodbyes. As I hugged each one of them, I knew that this was probably the last time that I would ever see them again. Many of them were returning home to Bosnia and others were trying to get selected to go to America, Australia or New Zealand. As we all gathered in front of a rows of buses, uncertain for what's next, we just hugged each other and cried uncontrollably. But as heartbroken as I was to leave my friends behind, I couldn't help but feel anxious and excited for all things that I knew were coming our way. I wanted to create my own American dream, and this was finally it, we were on our way!

The bus took us to Zagreb where we met up with our aunt from Slovenia to say our goodbyes. She gifted us with some food and a $100 bill. It was all that she had to give us, and we were very thankful. As we made our way to the airport, everything seemed so grand and over the top. We had never flown before or even seen a plane this big up close. It's ironic that now I'm terrified of flying but at that time, I wasn't. Despite never having flown before. I guess our excitement for the future overcame our fear. At some point during the flight, I thought the plane's wing was a mountain and I kept asking my mother why we were circling this mountain for nine hours. Silly kid.

WELCOME TO AMERICA

We had just landed at the Detroit Metro Airport as Bosnian refugees settling into America. In a small van packed with family members and a social worker, who was assigned to us to help with translating, we drove through the streets of Detroit headed to our new house in Hamtramck, Michigan. Nothing looked as I had expected. I snuggled up to my mother and asked if we were really in America. She turned to me and said, "Yes, this is America honey." As a kid growing up in Bosnia, I occasionally caught an episode of Beverly Hills 90210 and was fascinated by the big, beautiful white homes and palm trees. I'd never seen anything like that in person, so I had imagined America as this magical place where we'd live just like Brenda and Brandon Walsh.

Driving through Detroit I was waiting to see these big homes and palm trees, but it never happened. All I saw were small row homes, rundown buildings and dirty snow. Lots of it. "Sorry, little Vildana, no palm trees here," whispered my mom. We arrived in front of a small, gray house on Charest Street and the social worker told us this was where we'd be living with another family. We didn't care that we had to share a space with someone, we were just happy to be here.

All refugees had to go through many thorough physicals to check for any illness and diseases and were informed by our social worker that we'd spend the next day in a hospital getting all our shots up to date. I was twelve years old at the time, a couple of weeks' shy of my thirteen birthday. Man, I missed my friends. Just couple of days ago we were together in the camps, playing, laughing, and now we were scattered across the world.

Me and my siblings were placed in school according to our age. I was in seventh grade; my sister was in ninth grade and my brother was in third grade. Throughout refugee camps, we all went to school whenever it was offered to us, me basically skipping a part of 4th, 5th and 6th grade. The scariest part about being in a new country was not speaking the English language. I wanted to know what was being said around me and I wanted to communicate with my classmates, but I couldn't. Hamtramck was a city inside of Detroit, it's the only city inside of another city in the United States. It was filled with immigrants, thousands of people from all over the world struggling with this new life just like us. There was also a big Bosnian population so me and my siblings made friends quickly. We even got reunited with a few friends from the camps who ended up being sent here. I was determined to learn English as quickly as possible because I didn't want to stand out or be different, I just wanted to be "American". During the entire summer before 8th grade, my siblings and I spent our days playing Sega Genesis, eating ice cream and watching TV. We loved Family Matters because Steve Urkel was funny, but we couldn't understand the words. We kept the subtitles on and a dictionary nearby. That's basically how we learned to speak English. Along with some of our other favorite shows like Mama's Family.

In our middle school, all of the ESL (English as Second Language) classes were held in the basement and the first floor of the school. "Regular classes" were up on the top floor. Once our speaking skills got better, we would get moved to the top floor with the rest of the kids. I just remember saying to myself how much I wanted to be a regular American kid on the top floor, so I worked hard to make sure I was there once I started eighth grade.

That first year of school was hard for us. American kids would pick on the newcomers over our shoes, clothing or anything else that was different. We didn't know about brands or style; we were just happy to actually have clothing of our own. Over time, I became so angry I was being singled out that I just wanted to be "American". That became my mission. I didn't want anyone to know I had just come from Bosnia or the refugee camps, or that I was an immigrant. I just wanted to be a regular American girl, and in my mind, the first thing for me to do was to get rid of my accent.

In Bosnian schools, you'd get in trouble if you didn't say good morning to the teachers as they passed you in the hallway. Any slight sign of disrespect was punishable. I was so shocked when I started seeing how American kids treated teachers and how they behaved in school. I couldn't believe this was allowed - the cursing, fighting, and straight disrespect. It wasn't long after I started high school that I became one of those kids. My parents always ran a strict household. We were always expected to excel in school, never talk back and follow the rules. But once we moved to the states, it wasn't hard for me to get away with hiding suspension letters and bad grades since my parents weren't speaking English. My parents also worked a lot. My mom got a job at the pickle factory and my dad found work as a welder. I quickly started running with the wrong crowd so the skipping school and smoking became my new normal. Not too far from our high school were the neighborhood projects. That was our usual hangout spot, during or after school. One night, while hanging out inside of my friend's apartment, drinking, smoking, there was a shooting nearby. We found ourselves on the floor as the shots rang out and it all took me back to my childhood. I suddenly realized that I was headed down a wrong path. I came to the United States to avoid guns and violence yet there I was hanging out with the wrong crowd dodging bullets like I was in a war zone.

I was always heavily involved in sports; I was just naturally athletic. In high school, I played basketball, volleyball, softball and was a cheerleader. But over time as my attitude in school changed and my grades started slipping, so did my interest in extracurricular activities. I started not showing up to practice or even worse, when I was there, I'd be high, goofing off and not paying attention. As time went on, I stared quitting sports, one by one, and eventually wasn't involved in anything after school. My high school experience was quickly falling apart.

By the time I started tenth grade, my parents had somehow saved enough money to purchase a small home in Clinton Townships, a suburb north of Detroit. I was pissed. I did not want to leave my friends in Hamtramck. Just as I was getting comfortable in a new city, here we are moving again, just like in the camps. But my parents convinced us that the schools were better and that we were going to make new friends eventually.

Moving out of Hamtramck ended up being one of the best things that my parents had ever done for me, outside of moving us to the States. I am pretty sure I wouldn't have graduated high school if I had stayed in Hamtramck and if I'd continued the life I was living. Once I started my new school, I realized just how different I was, once again. I hated the way I spoke and was always super uncomfortable speaking in public. I had a thick Bosnian accent with some slang mixed in - it was horrible. Every day in school I would pray that teachers didn't call on me because I was so embarrassed, so I shut down.

My grades had gotten better than in my previous school, but I was still completely out of it when it came to my studies. All I wanted to do was graduate and get out of school. I figured I would just coast for the rest of my time in school and worry about everything else later. Not having a mentor or anyone that I could look up to was especially hard for me. I believed that if someone was there to guide me, I would've been more inspired about my future. At that time, I felt so lost, with no desires or plans to pursue anything past graduation. I had never dated much in high school. Being the new girl in this new school was kind of cool for a little bit but I never paid much attention to the boys. That was until I met my first real boyfriend Phil. He was so cute, and the closest thing I had to a high school "sweetheart". He was older than me and already out of school. That didn't work out too well as he was always involved in some shady business, so we ended it during my junior year. I was heartbroken, but I kept myself busy and stayed out of trouble. The summer before my senior year, I got myself a job at Burger King and Wendy's to make extra cash for my senior year costs. I would work the breakfast shift at Burger King from 5am to11am and then at Wendy's from 1pm to 9pm. My family was more financially stable than how we were the first few years in America, but if we wanted anything outside of "bare necessities" … we had to work for it. Allowance … what's that?

Senior year came around and all I wanted to do was finish school as quickly as possible and get out of there. I had no dreams or goals, no mentors and no direction. My communication with my parents was down to a minimum because I always felt that they didn't understand what I was going through. Despite living in America, their views on life remained very old school. They never had "the sex talk" with us or given us advice on how to deal with relationships, heartbreak, or even friendships. Over the years, my sister and I had completely grown apart. We were far from our childhood days in Bosnia when we spent almost every moment together. My sister was always the perfect kid with the perfect grades and perfect attitude. My brother was also a young teenager, but he had his own crowd, so I always felt I was on my own. Any teenage issues that I had, I was expected to just deal with it by myself. There was nobody to turn to. I had to learn everything through trial and error. Nobody was there to tell me about how men should treat women or to warn me about cheating and dishonesty. One night while I was out with friends, I met a cute guy named Randy. He was a little short, but he had beautiful, long black hair and these beautiful eyes. His dad was African American and his mom was Asian. It was the end of my senior year so when prom came around, Randy said that he didn't want to go because he was way older and thought that it would be a little weird. I decided to go without a date with a group of my girlfriends. He told me he'd meet up with me after prom. My best friend at the time, Fenise was pregnant and since we were all going to be together, I figured that we wouldn't be out late. I agreed. I had plenty of time to meet Randy. I had already lied my parents that I was staying at Fenise's house. The funny thing that ended up happening was that Fenise and I were wearing the exact same dress!!! We had never checked in with each other beforehand, so there we were going to the prom together...in the exact same dress. Child what a mess. I grabbed a quick bite to eat after prom and then Randy came to pick me up at the restaurant. We still had not had sex and I suppose that since it was prom, he thought it was about to go down. I liked Randy and I wanted to spend time with him, but for some reason, I still wasn't ready to give it up. Even though, "we're spending a night at the hotel after prom" was definitely a queue for the get-down – but I wasn't interested. As we made our way into the hotel room, I made it clear to him that nothing was going to happen. I just wanted to hang out. His intentions were elsewhere and he got so mad and took me home. When I walked into the house, my mother asked me why I'm home so early because she thought that I was spending the night with Fenise. I told her that I didn't feel like staying out and they I wanted to sleep in my bed. I took off my horrid clear and gold shoes, threw my dress in the closet and put on my favorite sweats. I laid on my bed and let out a big sigh as if to say, "Can high school be over already?"

THE EARLY STRUGGLE

After high school, I applied to Macomb Community College to study Communications. I just needed to do something since my parents told me that as long as I lived under their roof, I'd have to either pay rent or go to school. It was the summer of 2002. My sister was working at a local dentist office and had agreed to help me get a dental assistant job while I attended community college. It would also give me time to figure out what I wanted to do with my life. It wasn't a great fit seeing that I hated blood and couldn't stand the dentist ever since my horrible, no-anesthesia incident in the camp. I took the job anyway. I figured I could use $7.50 an hour for 20 hours a week. That would get me by. I was one month into the job before I realized I couldn't take it anymore, but I didn't want to quit and let my sister down. So, I spent most of my days dodging work and hanging out in the common area near the x-ray room. Thankfully, there was a radio there, so I would listen to Kris Kelly on my favorite radio station, FM 98 WJLB. It was a heritage hip hop/r&b radio station in Detroit and I had loved it since I came to America. I listened to it religiously, even recording songs on cassette tapes and falling in love with their on-air personalities. That's how I fell in love with hip hop and r&b, the first time I heard it on WJLB. We weren't exposed to American music in Bosnia or the refugee camps, only learning about Backstreet Boys and Spice Girls through the teen magazines that we read. But once I heard Puff Daddy and Lil' Kim… I was hooked. I'd spend time after school listening to Biggie, Mase and other artists … trying to write down their lyrics and translate them to Bosnian. I loved everything about hip hop and its culture. I was fascinated. Listening to Lil' Kim's Hardcore album in the car with my parents was pretty dope since they didn't speak English and had no idea what she was saying! I remember getting my heart broken in the 9th grade when I learned that Tupac had been killed. While I was talking about how much I loved him in front of a group of kids, one of them turned to me and said "you do know he's dead right?!!" … I was like what!!!!!! Totally shocked! How was I suppose to know that he wasn't here any more, I had just started learning about the culture. Safe to say I was heartbroken for a while, knowing that I'd never get a chance to see him in concert or better yet, meet him in person.

Earlier in the year on my 18th birthday, I called into WJLB to talk to Ludacris, one of my favorite artists at the time, who was in town for a show that night. I had already bought my tickets, so I really just called in to talk to him. It would be my first real concert ever. Local radio host Reggie Reg was on the air and he put me through to Luda who asked if I was coming to his show. "Yes…and it's my eighteenth birthday! I can't wait to see you!" I exclaimed.

To which he replied, "Oh, so you're grown now, you gonna wear your birthday suit to the show?"

I replied, "No, I was just gonna wear jeans and cute top." Clearly, I was not hip to the American lingo yet. I told him this story years later when I interviewed him on my show and we had a good laugh about it.

One day during Kris Kelley's lunch mix she mentioned that she was looking for interns. The interns had to be enrolled in college but there was no other experience necessary. Perfect! This caught my attention, so I quickly grabbed the phone and called in to find out where I could apply. Not sure why I was so eager to even pick up the phone. I took a radio class in high school and hated it. I never understood why anyone would want to sit in a small room and talk into a microphone to people you couldn't even see. But for some reason, this was different. I was excited. Earlier in the year, I had emailed Big Tigger who was hosting the morning show at WJLB at the time, to ask for advice for young students heading to college. The email bounced back. He was no longer there so I let it go.

There was an open casting call that week for an internship position and I made sure I was there. Dressed in my best professional clothing, I showed up feeling super confident. Since I was having a rough summer, this was definitely a new direction and the spark that I needed. After walking into the radio station lobby, my confidence quickly wavered when I saw the thirty other kids in the lobby, waiting for the same intern spot. I had to think quickly about what I could do to stand out otherwise, I'd be back to square one of nothingness. Once my name was called, I was led into Kris Kelley's office. I'd never seen anything like it. There were shelves on each side of the room with nothing but CDs and vinyl records in alphabetical order. There were platinum plaques everywhere, autographed photos of artists on the walls, trophies and awards on the shelves, and a bottle of champagne along with beautiful flowers on the desk. I thought to myself, this lady is living it up. A beautiful, petite woman with a huge smile turned around in her chair and greeted me. It was Kris Kelley, just as I had imagined her to be, by her radio voice. She started looking over my paperwork that I had been clenching in my hand for the past two hours. My list of interests was pretty short, and I could already tell I wasn't impressing her with anything that I had written down. When she looked up, she asked me what I saw for myself in the future. I immediately just started crying. I couldn't keep it together… I couldn't help it. I had nothing. I had no dreams, no goals, no social life, no normal home life, no interest in anything. Nothing. I was nothing.

I'm not sure if she just felt sorry for me or she actually had a real interest in what I was experiencing internally, but she asked me to go on. So I did, telling her everything I was feeling. I sat there and told her my entire history. The Bosnian life, the refugee camps, our transition to America and how I was trying to find my way. With tears rolling down my face and my voice breaking, I told her that I just didn't see the future and had no idea what I wanted to do. She was in awe. She gave me a hug and told me that it was all going to be okay. Realizing that I had probably just blew my chance at an internship, I quickly tried to gather myself together hoping to salvage anything left. Kris told me that she loved my honesty and that alone deserved a shot. The job was mine. She informed me that the internship was only three months long and unpaid, but I didn't care. I happily accepted the offer.

My first day at the radio station was October 22, 2002. I spent the day mostly organizing CD's, filing winners' information and getting coffee for the staff. After a week, it got pretty boring, but I figured there had to be some exciting things just around the corner. At this point, I had already quit the dentist office job and was working at Walgreens as a cashier overnight from 11p.m. to 7 a.m. My internship was from 10 a.m. to 3 p.m. I squeezed a few college classes in there sometimes, but most of the times, I didn't even attend. I wasn't really all that interested. At the time, I thought community college was just a lamer version of high school. I couldn't stand it, but I had to go at least sometimes, just so that my parents would let me live with them. But the schedule was killing me, I was barely getting any sleep.

One day the producer of the afternoon Reggie Reg show, Kapri, invited me to sit in on the show and see for myself all the things that happened behind the scenes on-air. Since I hadn't done much besides filing paperwork and getting coffee, I thought this would be exciting. Once I walked into the studio, I realized just how different this radio life was from what I had imagined it to be during my high school radio class. It was amazing! The music was blasting, live DJs, news, traffic, energy! There were artists waiting outside of the studio for an interview. There was so much going on! I sat in the corner and just observed everything around me, taking it all in, processing it. I started to picture myself behind the mic, actually doing that interview. But I could never do that, I thought to myself. I was too afraid of public speaking plus who would want to listen to me? My Bosnian accent was still pretty thick plus my slang wasn't helping either. I knew that if I ever wanted to pursue something like this, it would take a lot of work. One day while chatting with Kapri, as she was prepping for the afternoon show, she told me "I think me and you should definitely try to be radio personalities." I quickly dismissed it, laughing it off and going on about my business that day but it always stuck with me. Could I? My internship was quickly coming to an end and I felt like I hadn't really done much to advance or figure out my future plans. One day I got called into the office and I knew exactly what it was about. It was time to discuss my departure. As I sat in the chair waiting for Kris Kelley to walk in, I started thinking of all these different ways I was going to convince her to let me stay. As soon as she walked in, having no chance to even say a word, I calmly turned to her and said, "I'm not leaving." She was pretty shocked. Everything stopped for a moment. " I'm not leaving and y'all are just going to have to figure out what to do with me. I have nothing,." That's all I said and she just kinda gave me this look, like she was looking at a disobedient child, and shook her head.

Thankfully for me, I made friends with the promotions director at the time, Doddy Johnson. Doddy took me under her wing as she sensed that I was lost and needed guidance. She offered me a part-time promotions assistant job that paid $10 per hour, 15 hours a week. She didn't want to see me leave after my internship and wanted me to keep my foot in the door and that I would hopefully figure out the rest. I obviously took the job and was super excited. One day, while working on a big promotion for WJLB's annual charity event, I had a chance to interact with the listeners of the station and see the interaction they had with the on-air personalities. It was so much love all around. They were like rock stars to them - community heroes! That's when I finally realized that this was what I truly wanted to do, to be an on-air personality. To connect with the people and to earn their trust. To bring them that joy and excitement that I saw that day. Yes, that's what I wanted to be. Finally I had a vision!!!

My next step was to figure out how to actually get on-air. KJ Holiday was the program director of WJLB, the boss, the man that made all the decisions. He was a very well-respected program director who had been in the radio game for many many years. His personality was warm but very stern when it came to business. He would eventually become one of my mentors but at the time, every time I'd mention my "on air dream" he'd just brush me off as one of the promotions assistants that probably wouldn't stick around long enough. But I was determined. I came up with a plan. First, I needed to work on my voice delivery and my accent. Because I was a promotions assistant, I had access to other parts of the studio around the station. Whenever a studio was available, and I had free time, I'd go in and record myself talking. Sometimes I would read commercial scripts or books, anything I could get my hands on that would help me work on my voice. Then I would take that tape and have one of the real on-air personalities listen to it, most of the time their reaction was "you sound like shit" but I kept at it. I also needed to get some on air experience in a small market, all while still keeping my foot at WJLB. I remembered a girl by the name of Jazzy T who worked in Lansing Michigan at a small radio station by Michigan State University. She told me that they would be hiring soon and that this could be a great way to start my career. The only issue was that it was two hours away and I wasn't quite sure that my hooptie car could make that trip every week. But I still did what I had to do.

The program director at that station was hard to reach so I called him every single day during that summer of 2003 until he finally picked up and said, "Damn, you're determined".

He agreed to finally meet with me and check out my air-check. I was soooooo nervous. I got myself ready, put on my best business attire and headed to Lansing, Michigan. It was a cold October day, 2003. The entire ride there, I just prayed that the heat in my car wouldn't cut off and that I would make it safely to Lansing. I didn't have much money in my bank account, but I figured it was worth the drive and the gas money. When I got to Power 96.5, it was pretty small, nothing like WJLB in Detroit. It turns out, there was a huge difference in the Lansing market #159 and the

Detroit market #10. I didn't care, all I could think about was how I could impress this program director, so he would put me on the air. I never expected what happened next! It was around 1:30pm and we were just chatting in his office about my radio goals and my experience at WJLB, when all of a sudden, he received a phone call from his afternoon radio host that was due on air in 30 minutes. Apparently, he had an emergency and wasn't going to make it to work. There was nobody else there to cover his shift, so the Program Director looked at me and said, "Get ready to show me what you got!" I was blindsided! My anxiety kicked in and my mind was racing. *Omg, omg, omg! He wants me to go on-air right now? By myself? To actually talk to people? By myself?* I. Was. Panicking.

Somehow, I calmed down and turned my panic into confidence. "For sure, I can hold it down" I said and I did. I already knew how to work the studio equipment since that was the first thing they teach you in the radio world. My brain was scattered, but I gathered myself enough to remember the things my mentors taught me at WJLB and made the show my own that afternoon. I created a playlist, had a gossip report, a small mix at 5p.m. I basically took all the things I saw in Detroit and remixed it into this show.

I guess I did a decent job because I was offered a Sunday on-air shift from 12pm to 5pm. Yes! I was excited! My first on-air gig! I didn't care that it paid $6.50 per hour, was only 5 hours a week and was a two-hour-drive each way. I figured that $32.50 minus tax was enough to get me from Clinton Township (my parents' house) to Lansing, weekly. This didn't sit well with my parents. They were already on to me that I was skipping my college classes. Not to mention, they weren't too thrilled that I was going into radio in the first place. "You're really going to spend an entire Sunday somewhere making 30 bucks hoping you make it big on the radio? Does anyone even listen in Lansing?" said my mother. I didn't care. Something in me said that this would eventually pay off and I actually believed that voice inside of me. I had the freedom to do the show however I pleased, to arrange songs however I wanted and to talk about whatever topics I so chose –so I went for it. Some shows were good, and some were pretty terrible. But I got better, and I kept on working. One cold Sunday in December, I gathered my things and headed to Lansing to do my show. I usually left at 9am just to make sure I got there by noon. It only took couple of hours but I'd always been super obsessed with being on time. I even lost friends who were constantly so late that I felt disrespected and I had to cut them off. I know, very dramatic. As I did every morning, I said a small prayer once I got in my car, mostly because my hooptie was at the end of its rope and could die on me at any moment. I wasn't trying to get stranded on I-96 in the middle of winter so I figured if God was with me, everything would be fine. An hour into the drive and the snow was coming down pretty hard. It was a typical Michigan winter. I turned up my heat and my windshield wipers – only for the wipers to not work. Holy shit, I couldn't see! What else can go wrong with this fuckin car? Somehow, I managed to pull over, and without getting hit by the other cars flying by me and cleaned off my windshield with my sleeve since I couldn't find my snow cleaner. I did this for the next few miles, stopping every so often when I could barely see anymore and cleaning my car because I had to get to work. There was no other option. I couldn't call my parents because this would be just another reason for them to say how I was wasting my time, driving this far for no money in the snow. I finally arrived at the station, 5 minutes before my show started. My coat was wet and dirty from all the snow I'd been cleaning off my car for the past few miles, while I was praying I wouldn't die. But once I walked in the studio and put my headphones on and the "ON AIR" light came on, all the bullshit that I'd just endured for the past three hours was gone. That's when I knew that I truly loved radio.

My parents were young and in love! Not sure about this baby basket but my sister is in there somewhere. Summer 1982, Bosnia.

This is one of my favorite photos of my father, my sister and I. As you can tell from our worn-out yellow boots, we loved to play outside... nonstop. Loved the pixie cuts too! Winter 1988, Bosnia.

My mother often dressed me and my sister in matching clothing ... and haircuts! Summer 1990, Bosnia.

One of my fondest memories of our babysitter/ third grandma Dzejo was her always feeding us fresh mozzarella cheese and her warm hands. She always wore many hijabs on her head at the same time. Fall 1984, Bosnia.

In 2013 I visited my step-grandmothers home after being away for 19 years. It brought back so many memories. We loved this house and everything it stands for. My mother also grew up in this house.

My one and only photo from Turanj refugee camp, sitting with my cousin at our makeshift house that my father just finished building for us. Fall 1994, Croatia

Our aunt visiting us in Gasinci refugee camp. The trailers were so crammed and every person had to keep all of their belonging at the edge of your bed. Summer 1996, Croatia.

We loved spending time outside, even in the refugee camps. I was also an avid reader, whenever I can get my hands on a book. Summer 1996, Croatia.

We loved catching the bus out of the refugee camp and into a nearby Croatian city. We'd walk around, get ice cream and teen magazines. Trying to be normal teenagers. Fall 1996, Croatia.

We often gathered in one of the refugee camp trailers to host girls' nights. It would get really cold so we used blankets on the walls to keep the cold air from coming in. Winter 1996, Croatia.

I loved going to the mosque in the refugee camp. It would take away all of my worries and circumstances and connect me to God. I'm photo'd here in a black hijab. Winter 1996, Croatia.

Me and my sister Dina at 14 and 15 years old. Someone must've made me mad that day lol. Summer 1998, Hamtramck MI.

My best friend Rian and I were inseparable in our late teens/early twenties. Someone tell me to throw away that bleach blonde hair and the blazer. Yikes. Winter 2004, Detroit MI.

We were charged a "travel fee" to come into America as refugees. You had to get job immediately and start paying it back. It was our first debt to America before we even stepped a foot onto the soil. Spring 1997, Hamtramck MI.

Bushman was one of the first people to believe in me and mentor me throughout my start in radio. Here's us at my first Coats for Kids charity event. Winter 2002, Detroit MI.

Whenever I could, I'd sneak in the studio and pretend that I was a real radio host. I'd also practice my autograph and imagine what it would be like if I made it big. Winter 2003, Detroit MI.

As a promotions coordinator at the age of 20, I was so excited to have an office. It had a window that lead to an alley so I covered it with photos of Miami to make it seem like I was on the beach. Summer 2004, Detroit MI.

THE MAN AND THE GRIND

I didn't have much of a personal life. The summer after I graduated high school, on the fourth of July, I met this beautiful man, Dee (we'll call him that for now). Me and my girlfriends were headed to the beach which was a few miles from our parents' house in Clinton Twp. There was a huge accident and the entire road to the beach was shut down, so we got diverted to I-94 which we took straight to downtown Detroit. We were all eighteen years old and didn't really know much of what was happening on the "social scene" at the time, but since I had my car, I figured we'd just drive around. I stopped at a gas station to fill up, but I couldn't use my debit card because my nails were too long. Just as I was getting frustrated at the pump, this man at the next pump came over to help me. At first, I didn't even look him in the face, which wasn't unusual for me. My thoughts and eyes usually glaze over strangers as I keep the conversation short and sweet. But this time, as he was helping me, our eyes locked and I realized just how fine he was. He was a bit taller than me (I'm 5'5) but he had a nice smile and beautiful eyes, not to mention, he looked like he spent all his free time at the gym. After a quick chat, I learned that he lived in Florida and was in town visiting family for the holiday.

I assumed he was in Florida for college, so we exchanged numbers and headed our separate ways. A month went by before we spoke again. I learned he was living in Tampa, playing for the Tampa Bay Buccaneers and that he was five years older than me. Over the next few years, we shared an on and off relationship. We were both very much involved in our careers. All I wanted to do was radio and he was pretty busy with football. Obviously, he was super successful, and I was super struggling, but I never wanted him to know that. So whenever I was around him, I made sure to tell him stories of how great everything in my life was because I never wanted him to know that I needed him for anything, other than simply him. I'd always been weird about money. I could never ask for it and I did everything in my power to make the people that I love know I'm okay, so that they didn't have to worry about me, despite being down to my last dime. That relationship wasn't destined to go anywhere because I could never be myself around him. I had to pretend to be "poppin" so he would know that I had my own and wasn't after his money. Even though I was driving my hooptie to Lansing every weekend for $32.50, I made him think that I had this great dope job that was taking me places. On some level, I think he knew my situation. He even gave me money at times, but my pride was just too much. I wanted to create a life for myself that was so great, that any man that came along would just be an amazing addition to my life. I knew early on that I didn't want a relationship where I had to solely depend on someone else to take care of me.

2004 was a big year for me. I finally moved up from the Promotions Assistant position to a Promotions Coordinator. It was my first salaried position and of course, I was ecstatic! First thing, I did was move out of my parents' house. By this time, I had dropped out of college to completely give my 100% to radio. Things had gotten out of hand with working promotions at WJLB, going to college and driving to Lansing for my weekend shift at Power 96.5, so I quit my weekend shift too! I quit it all for WJLB. There I was, twenty years old, in a manager position with a staff of five. Things were looking up.

Even though I was an extrovert, I was also a loner. I loved being alone and in my thoughts. I guess you can call that a Social Loner. I'd always been very independent and self-sufficient, so it wasn't a huge shock to my parents that I wanted to move into my own place as soon as I started to make some type of money. I didn't leave because my parents were strict or because I wanted to have parties or boys over at the house. I just wanted to be alone and independent. I guess underneath it all, I wanted to prove to my family that I could do it. "Look Ma, I'm finally making money in radio and I can live by myself." Nowadays, I always urge kids to stay at home as long as they can and save their money. For the first few years all I did was work nonstop to even afford the place I lived in, despite the rent being just $550 in Detroit. I spent so much time working I never even got to enjoy my place.

2004.... the Detroit Pistons had just won the NBA Champions beating the Los Angeles Lakers. The entire city of Detroit erupted as people were celebrating in the streets and I could hear it all from my 16th floor apartment. I kept my windows open most of the time when the weather was warm. I had a small studio apartment, probably the size of my bedroom at the parents' house, with a small kitchen and even a smaller bathroom. I thought it was cute since it was close to work and it had floor to ceiling windows. My view of downtown Detroit's skyline was worth the rent. My friends were texting me asking if I wanted to join them in the celebration at a bar nearby. I wasn't even old enough to drink but that didn't stop me. I knew every bartender and club owner in the city and most of them wouldn't say no to me. I declined and decided to sit in silence in my apartment, taking in the city noise as the sun was setting. I've always been a little weird like that, even when I was a little kid. Infatuated with the moon and the stars, sun and the air. I could spend hours gazing at the stars. It took me back to the days in Bosnia when we would stargaze on the balcony of our house, while my mother would peel apples and share her childhood stories. Memories. As I sat by myself, gazing at the city filled with so much life and excitement, I felt very empty. I started thinking about how I'd never had a real high school sweetheart relationship, how I dropped out of college and missed out on the ultimate college experience. I'd heard so many times that they were the best years of your life. I thought about how I was working nonstop to live paycheck to paycheck. There was no man in my life that loved me. I was alone. Then I started thinking about my boss, Kris Kelley. I admired her so much, she had everything I'd ever wanted –an amazing job, beautiful house, Range Rover, money to spend, but she was alone. Though

I was certain, she had an amazing dating life, she didn't have a husband or any kids. So to me, that meant, she's alone and lonely. I didn't know much about her family life; I just knew she was from Philly. And just like her, I had moved away from my family as soon as I was able to. As those thoughts rushed through my head, I actually closed my eyes and mumbled to myself, "God, please don't let me end up like Kris Kelley, I don't want to end up alone".

Things in radio that year got pretty hectic. I was juggling my Promotions Coordinator position and a weekend on-air spot at WJLB! Holy shit! Yes! My station gave me an on-air spot on the weekend. It wasn't much extra money than what I was already making as Promo Coordinator but just being on air, even if it's part-time on the weekend was a big deal. That experience is unmeasurable. So basically, I was working seven days a week. Soon it was time to celebrate my 21st birthday. I wasn't even too excited about it because I was already getting into 21+ places so to me it was just another year! But I decided to join some friends at a place down the street called St. Andrews. St. Andrews was a legendary spot in Detroit where many got their start in hip hop, from Eminem, D12 and more. It was known for hosting all the dopest shows, especially from up and coming and underground artists. My first time seeing Kanye West was at St. Andrews the year before. I had met him previously as he was just a new artist and he was very polite. I remember him sitting in a studio with his girlfriend, Alexis at the time, covered in blankets because we kept the studios very cold. Later on, he would perform at St. Andrews so the entire station was there. The whole place went completely dark when the small stage in front of us, lit up with people dressed in white. Kanye performed Jesus Walks.

It was one of the dopest experiences I could remember at St. Andrews, outside of when Eminem and Jay-Z performed and a few girls in the front row fainted from excitement. The ambulance had to be called and it was a mess. Detroit loved them some Eminem. It was only right that I celebrate my birthday at St. Andrews with some friends at the bar. One of those friends was Proof, a member of D12 group who were pretty big in Detroit and had been a part of Eminem's crew for a long time. Drinks were flowing. Finally, I was old enough to legally drink. I was having a great time and then - BAM! All I felt was an airbag in my face! What just happened? It was like a dream and then suddenly I woke up startled by a hard hit to the face by my airbag and the smell of gasoline. I looked up and realized that I had been driving already for a few minutes, not even realizing, and ran full speed into a parked truck on a one-way street. I lived just a few blocks over from St. Andrews and this one-way street was usually how I got home. The entire front of my car was totaled and I was squeezed in the front seat with not much room. I was by myself. The street was dark and one way, so there were no cars coming or going. I was the only car (along with the packed truck) on the street. Holy shit what do I do now? I can't go to jail on my 21st birthday. Besides, I had just gotten this car with the little bit of the money I was making, and I couldn't afford to fuck this up. I somehow pried the door open and squeezed my body through the crushed metal. My white blazer was completely soaked in some weird green fluid and the gasoline was leaking from the vehicle as I crawled under the car to find my blackberry. Omg, am I going to die? I wondered. Is this car about to explode? What is my family going to say?? So many things went through my head as I sobered up quickly! "Can you please come get me, I was in an accident?" I screamed into my blackberry, my friend Jay was on the other line. He wasn't far away and was headed to pick me up, but he warned me to get as far away from the car as possible. I could not figure out how this just happened, we were all just standing at the bar having a great time.

Who would let me leave knowing how fucked up I was? I started getting angry, but I was still so inebriated that I no longer was paying attention to the car I hit (which wasn't damaged much) or my own gasleaking car as it just sat completely totaled on the street. Jay came around the corner in his escalade, scooped me off the ground and said, "I can't' let you go to jail on your birthday." We completely left the scene.

The next few days were awful. I wanted to blame my friends for letting me drive, knowing I was so fucked up, but the story that I learned shocked me even more. Every single friend I talked to told me that I seemed completely fine. I talked to everyone, had a full-on conversation, even got on the mic couple of times. Yet, I didn't remember any of this, not even a blur. It was a complete blackout. They said that they walked me to my car, I said my goodbyes, even said bye to my cop friends who usually stand outside of St. Andrews patrolling the street. Nobody had any idea that I was completely blacked out while functioning like a normal person. So, I googled it. It was an actual thing. Yes. After a few drinks, your brain stops recording memory but you're functioning completely normal and nobody is able to tell that you've had "too much". What does that even mean? It felt very dangerous to me. I'd just turned 21 and now what? Maybe I shouldn't drink ever again, I thought.

I was always the person who believed that your pure happiness should be the number one thing on your list of priorities. Over money, over material things, jobs or anything else, there should be happiness. If you aren't happy in your relationship, leave. If you don't like your job, quit and find something else. Especially in your 20s. Those are the times to try every and anything once and see where it goes. Sitting in my office, one hot summer day of 2005, I realized just how much I hated being the Promotions Coordinator. Why couldn't they give me a full time on-air shift? I'd been there for nearly three years and had worked my way up from an intern, to producer, to promotions assistant to promotions coordinator.

All while doing my on-air Sunday shift, but that wasn't enough. All I wanted to do was be an on-air personality and nothing else. A month prior, I had just moved into a beautiful townhouse in Dearborn, right next door to my best friend Rian. We've been best friends since the moment I met her at the radio station three years earlier, where she was trying to get an internship just like me at the time. And she did. But after a while she quit the internship to pursue her other passions. I loved her free spirit and beautiful heart. She came from a very close family that lived just a few miles from our Dearborn townhomes in Rosedale park on the West side of Detroit. Her mother was a beautiful brown skinned woman with the sweetest soul. She was a therapist so having conversations with her was always fun because I could never have those with my mother, especially about sex. Pretty sure I never said the word sex around my mother, let alone my parents until I was well into my late 20s. Her father was a sweet white man who was a very talented musician. Rian was a beautiful mix of both of her parents. I loved spending time with them, eventually even calling her mother, MOM (My Other Mother). With this new townhouse, I knew that despite hating my Promotions Coordinator position, I had to keep working because I simply wasn't making any money doing just my Sunday on-air shift. I managed to somehow get through the summer, but the station quickly realized that I simply wasn't being productive (and hated) my Promotions Coordinator job and they let me go. They allowed me to keep my weekend on-air shift, but I needed to quickly figure out what I was going to do next as far as making real money. Not going to lie,

I was eyeing the strip club for two seconds, before realizing that it would never work for me. The radio station was hosting a huge party at St. Andrews every Friday night.

Bushman, who I used to intern for, told me I could be his assistant. As his assistant, I would be responsible for driving the station van to the party, hanging up the banners and setting up DJ equipment. The job paid $100 in cash I was up for it. Who wouldn't wanna hang out at the biggest Friday night party in the city and make some money?

But it wasn't all that I expected it to be. During the party, I'd usually run back and forth from the DJ to the host to make sure our broadcast was on air and that we were staying on time. After the party, I'd be the last person to leave as I'd have to take apart all the equipment, put it back in the truck, carry it upstairs to the radio station, before returning the station's truck back to the garage. For what I thought was going to be a fun 4-hour job, turned into 8 and it wasn't THAT fun. There was no popping bottles and standing on couches. This was work! But I didn't mind doing the dirty work, I just really needed that money. Plus, now that I was out of the full time job as a Promotions Assistant, I needed to find full time employment during the week in order to continue to live on my own.

THE BIG BREAK

It always made me happy to know that my loved ones weren't worried about me. I would go to any length to make sure that they thought I was fine. Even if I had to lie about how my life was going, if I had to paint that pretty picture for them, I'd do it. As a middle child, in so many ways, even as I was growing up, I was always extremely independent. To me, I always wanted everyone around me to think that I had it "all together", even when I didn't. My parents were the best parents a kid could ask for. They provided a roof over our heads, food on the table, and clothes on our backs. Everything after that was up to us. We never even had allowances growing up. We didn't have the dope clothes or sneakers that we wanted. We had to find a way to get them. Otherwise, we had to rock whatever they gave us, which was whatever they could afford. My first job was when I was fourteen years old at a pizza spot around the corner from our house in Hamtramck. I was pretty sure they were doing some shady business out of there, but I didn't care. I wanted to earn enough money to buy my Air Max sneakers which at the time were around $200. After a few weeks, once I saved up my $200 for the sneakers, I quit. Quite honestly, I was tired of going to school smelling like onions every day for some sneakers.

In a way, my parents' disapproval and doubt gave me that extra push and motivation to succeed. It was almost like I always wanted to prove them wrong or to prove something to them. Everything I did or wanted to do came with an, "I told you I could do it", in the end. And if I failed, I knew that they weren't going to coddle me and tell me that everything would be okay. They would say, "We told you so." That was the relationship we had. I knew they hated my career path. In fact, they never thought that it was a good idea to get into the radio business. At first, they weren't fond of my internship and the fact that I wasn't making any money. No parent would! And let's not forget that I dropped out of college on three different occasions because I couldn't keep up with my studies, work numerous jobs and do my radio internship - but that nonpaying internship later turned into a career. I had no plan B or C, my plan A had to pay off for me because I was not going to allow myself fail. Basically my parents eventually pushed me to success because they were my biggest critics.

I landed myself a part time job at a nearby Arden B clothing store in the mall to make some extra money during the week, while I dedicated my weekends to radio. I had a Sunday show that aired from 10a.m. to 2p.m., making $10 per hour. That paycheck couldn't even buy me food for the week. I couldn't even afford to blast my heat in my apartment so the time I spent in my house I'd be under numerous blankets trying not to freeze to death. Health insurance? Nope, I couldn't afford to get sick because that was nonexistent. One time I had gotten sick but with $18 in my bank account, I couldn't afford the $120 medicine prescription from CVS. Thankfully, my best friend Rian agreed to loan me the money. Bless her heart, she knew that I had no way of paying her back, at least not anytime soon. I know it was an inconvenience for her since she wasn't making a lot of money at her job either. We were just a bunch of broke twenty-year-olds looking out for each other.

It was the middle of a cold Detroit winter. Everybody knows about those, even the outta towners would sing, "It's so coldddddd in the Deeeeeeee", whenever they met me. January in Detroit is not pleasant. Cold air hit my face as I slid under my blankets to walk over to the kitchen. My heat had been cut off for two days now as I pleaded with the heating company to give me an extension on my payment. I couldn't ask anyone for any more money because I was embarrassed. Besides, my sister had already given me money for rent a couple of months earlier. I promised that I would pay her back soon, knowing that I couldn't. As I walked around my apartment, so many thoughts flashed through my mind. "What the hell had I gotten myself into? My life could've been so much easier if I'd just listened to my family, went to school, followed the rules. But look at me. I'm poor, alone, no education, chasing some dream that may not happen and again... hella poor."

I started toying with the thought that everything would be easier if I just ended it all. Why not? I thought. I felt like I wasn't doing life "right", as though everything in my life had gone left and my only way out was to end it. I went into my bathroom and started looking through cleaning products. I didn't really know what I was looking for, but I knew I needed something strong. I thought, if I was going to kill myself, I may as well go all the way through with it. I didn't want someone to find me unconscious and think that I did it for attention. Even in the middle of a complete breakdown, I carried the burden of other people's reactions to what I was plotting, especially my family. I didn't want to suffer, I thought. I needed this to be fast. As I sat in the middle of my cold bathroom, I started reading the label on a bottle of bleach, but nowhere did I see that it would kill you immediately. As I was scrambling through these products, tears started flowing from my face. I started to think back to my childhood and all the beautiful memories that my family and I had created. I'd never have family dinners again or see my little brother grow up. I paused. I couldn't do it. At this point, the tears were uncontrollable. My body was so numb from the cold bathroom floor I was sitting on. Praying that I would find clarity and wake up with a whole new outlook on life, I curled up on that bathroom floor, with tears running down my face, and fell asleep.

Sundays were for family dinners at my parents' house. As I drove there, I knew that my mother was going to ask me why my face was so swollen. I had a complete meltdown and cried for hours the day before but obviously that wasn't the story I was going to tell her. Once she asked, I made up a lie saying I was sick and took a lot of NyQuil in order to fall sleep. I held back tears as I ate dinner. Family time wouldn't have happened if I had gone through with plans to end my life. As we made small talk about my job at the radio station, I assured them that of course everything was going perfectly fine. There was no way I could tell them that my entire world was crashing down and that I thought I was at the end of my rope. With no money and no food at my house, I packed a to-go plate and started to drive back to Dearborn from my parents' house. The roads were very icy that night and I felt myself sliding all over the freeway. I needed to slow down, but I could barely keep my eyes open. My face was still swollen from the night before as I fought back tears. I began crying uncontrollably again. My mind started racing a mile a minute as I thought this may be the end for me. Maybe I was supposed to die in some crash on the freeway during an ice storm so that way my family wouldn't think I did it to myself. Maybe it wasn't supposed to happen last night, maybe tonight is the perfect time for this. Make it look like an accident. I braced myself, this was it. Then, suddenly, out of nowhere – a song came on the radio… it was Carrie Underwood's "Jesus Take the Wheel". A sense of calm and peace immediately came over me as I turned the radio all the way up.

The song went

She was driving last Friday on her way to Cincinnati on a snow-white Christmas Eve

Going home to see her mama and her daddy with the baby in the backseat

Fifty miles to go, and she was running low on faith and gasoline

It'd been a long hard year

She had a lot on her mind, and she didn't pay attention

She was going way too fast

Before she knew it she was spinning on a thin black sheet of glass

She saw both their lives flash before her eyes

She didn't even have time to cry

She was so scared

She threw her hands up in the air

Jesus, take the wheel

Take it from my hands

'Cause I can't do this on my own

I'm letting go

So give me one more chance

And save me from this road I'm on

Jesus, take the wheel

94

Every single word she sang pierced through my heart... she was me and I was her. I needed to hear those exact words. Yes, for a Muslim like me, a song about Jesus saved my life that day. I was so broken and broke. But I took that song as a sign that God was still in my corner and that everything will be okay. This was my trying season and I was up for the challenge. I slowly wiped the tears away, sat up high, slowed down , got in the middle lane and drove home.

The next week I got evicted from my apartment and it happened in such a dramatic fashion – all I needed was one more week to gather up the rest of my rent money, but the leasing office was not trying to hear that. At the time, Rian was working full time at Chase Bank down the street and told me that she could get me a job that paid more than Arden B, and I would have my weekends free to continue working at the radio station. But technically, I was now homeless and didn't know where to turn. Thankfully, Rian allowed me to sleep on her couch while I was trying to figure out my next steps and she got me in Chase Bank. My parents never visited me in Dearborn, I'd always drive up to Clinton Township to see them, which made it easier for me to keep hiding the fact that I had gotten evicted. Sleeping on someone's couch is never easy, even if it is your best friend. The feeling of inconveniencing someone, walking around on tippy toes, and trying not to disturb their lives is very uncomfortable. I never wanted to be a burden, and I knew Rian never thought of me as one, but I thought that of myself. I had to get myself back on track – soon!

Fall came, and I realized that I just had to do the one thing that I've been avoiding – telling my family that I didn't have that fabulous full-time job at the station and that I needed to move back in. It was so hard for me. I was embarrassed. My parents never really said, "We told you so," but I felt it. My family wasn't really a "let's talk about our feelings today" type of family, so anytime there was a real issue to be discussed, it was terrifying. Nevertheless, I couldn't let their disappointment stop me from pursuing my dream. I figured that since I didn't have anything to lose, I would just keep working hard and eventually it would all pay off. It had to. If I put 200% to build my career, it couldn't fail because I wouldn't allow it to fail.

By this time, I had quit Chase bank and found myself a receptionist job at a real estate firm. I was working nine to ten hours a day. Over the summer, while I lived at Rian's house I had gained a lot of weight, mostly because I was working a lot and eating a lot of fast food along the way. Gym? What's that? I hadn't seen a gym in years. I had completely let myself go. Now that I was living back with my parents, working a full-time job, being an "upstanding citizen" and contributing to the household, I started taking care of myself better. Social life had completely slowed down for me because after working nine hours a day, who wants to drive all the way to Detroit to go out? Not me, I needed my full night of sleep. Plus, I was dieting heavy and working out in my parents' basement. Not many people knew that I was back living with my family, not even some family members. I didn't want anyone to feel sorry for me, so I spent most of my time in the basement, avoiding the chance to run into people that I didn't want to see. Bosnians could be very nosy, gossipy and judgmental. I knew there would be the question of "What happened to your big job and radio career in the city?". Mentally, I wasn't prepared to answer any questions or to even to be social at all…so I avoided it.

Moving back in with my parents and getting myself together was exactly what I needed. It was a blessing in disguise. During the winter, I dropped over twenty pounds. I was happier and feeling more enthusiastic about life. I enjoyed doing my Sunday radio show because I didn't expect or need much from it (money wise). At some point, I thought I might eventually phase out of radio. No new opportunities were coming, and my radio career was feeling a bit stale. I even enrolled into University of Michigan Dearborn Campus with hopes of finding a new career path, but I couldn't find anything I was interested in. After taking some general classes without any clear direction of where I wanted to go with it, I eventually ended up dropping out again. The classes were super expensive and definitely not in my budget. In a way, I may have taken those classes to make my parents happy, to show them that maybe I could go to school and eventually get my degree. But my heart was not in it.

Working at the real estate office was a huge change for me. I was responsible to arrive first, open the office, start the coffee, and prepare all the paperwork before the rest of the staff gets there. The year was 2007 and I had just created my Facebook profile. I'm pretty sure I was super late to the social media party but once I joined, I was hooked. I spent most of my free time at work on Facebook. On one particularly slow Friday morning, as I was browsing Facebook and my radio email, I noticed that I received a note from my radio boss, KJ Holiday, telling me to call him as soon as possible. Panic started to set in as I started thinking about what he could want from me. I haven't seen or heard from anyone at the radio station for a while, since nobody is there on Sundays and I never make it to staff meetings because I'm working my "day job". Did I fill out my timesheet card wrong or did I say something on air that I shouldn't? All these thoughts went through my head before I mustered up the courage to call him, fortyfive minutes later.

KJ: Sunshyne, how long have you been here at the station, going on five years now right?

Me: Yes, five years this October...

KJ: I know that you've been hustling since day one, and you've gotten pretty good at this radio stuff. I think we may have something big for you here …

Me: **complete panic**

KJ: Kris Kelley is leaving middays so Cheron from the Quiet Storm will be taking her spot…which means the Quiet Storm is yours … if you want it?

Me: **Silence. **

There were no words, I was screaming inside my head, pretty sure I'd passed out at some point from the lack of oxygen. He went on to say how they didn't have much money to offer me, but it was still a good salaried position and I would only work 4 nights a week, 10p.m.-2a.m. Full time salary job for sixteen hours a week, on the biggest radio station in Detroit? Fuck yeah, I'd take it! Somehow, I composed myself long enough to simply say: yes sir, I'll take it. Thank you so much.

I couldn't wait to tell my parents about the exciting news! That all this hard work that I had put in for the past five years had finally paid off. I was going to be a full-time radio personality, and nobody was going to take that joy away from me. I knew that I was going to get met with "Oh don't get too excited, you know what happened before". I didn't care, I was over the moon. All those years of working for pennies praying that it pays off was finally here. The long trips to Lansing for $30 per week just to be on-air for five hours for a handful of people that were even able to get that radio station's signal. The long days and nights working in the promotions department, hanging up banners, setting up equipment, dealing with crazy listeners and coworkers. Wow. It was really happening. I'd become friends with everyone at the real estate firm, so they were definitely happy for me, but also sad to see me go. I gave my two-week's notice the moment I got off the phone with KJ, I was ready to bounce up out of there. Soon after, I signed a two-year radio contract for the Quiet Storm at FM 98 WJLB. I was twenty-three years old. I became the youngest full-time radio host in the city and the only woman from my country to have that position on mainstream radio. History.

DETROIT RADIO

Working as the Quiet Storm host was a whole new life for me. Finally, I was making money doing what I love, and doing something that I worked and waited for, for so long. The first thing I did when I signed my contract was move out of my parents' house, again. I spent the next two years working as the Quiet Storm host. I was living back in downtown Detroit and I vowed to never move back home again. Those nine months back were enough! I worked Monday through Thursday from 10:00 p.m. to 2:00 a.m. I had weekends and Mondays off until 10 p.m. Life was golden. Parties, concerts, celebrity interviews, that was my day to day! There were times I still felt somewhat empty, as though I wasn't fulfilling my purpose, but I brushed it off. I continued to live the fast-paced life and work the social scene.

Finally, I was also in a relationship! I'd met J while I was out having one of my typical girls' nights out. I was the queen of those. Gathering up the girls and going out, having our own VIP table to drink and dance without any disruptions from men was everything to me. J was standing at the bar with one of his friends as I spotted him. Never being the one to approach a man, this time I couldn't help it. I walked up to him and said, "omg, you look just like NeYo!" – What? This man looked nothing like NeYo but I guess my nervousness took over and the words just came out. He laughed it off and we had a short conversation before exchanging numbers. He was seven years older than me and I really liked that. I've never been the one to date men who were younger or the same age. We spent our summer traveling to places like Vegas, Miami and St. Thomas, going to romantic dinners and simply enjoying each other's company. I had never been in such "good" situation, it was effortless. Maybe too effortless. One day while I was at work, I received an email from his account. First, I thought it was a confirmation for our upcoming trip because he would usually email me our itinerary. But it wasn't. It was an email from a woman claiming that she was his live-in girlfriend and that they had two kids together. I had no idea that he had children so to say I was shocked would be an understatement. The woman went on to mention that she knew about all of our trips and whereabouts. She also mentioned a few other trips that I didn't recognize but I kept reading. At the bottom of the email, it wasn't addressed to me, it was addressed to another woman. Wow. So, he had two side girls and a main. Wow, wow, wow. Thankfully, my boss, KJ walked in the studio around the time I got the email. With him being my long-time mentor, I asked him what I should do. He told me to not respond to that email and to quickly end this relationship. "Sunshyne, she can easily find you, your job, what you look like, everything… but you don't know her.

She can be outside right now waiting for you; you don't need this type of drama."

I took his advice and immediately ended my relationship with J. I didn't even tell him why, I just stopped answering his calls and texts. After a few days, he probably looked at his email account and figured it out. I've never been very confrontational in relationships, even friendships. It had always been very easy for me to completely dead a situation without thinking twice about it. Men have called me cold, ice queen, etc ... I don't care. My sanity and wellbeing were always my number one priority, especially since I had to take care of myself all the time. KJ taught me many lessons and had given me some great advice over the years. He told me that in the entertainment world, you always want to have women on your side. Women are everything, they make the household decisions and they control everything. You never want to be the woman that other women are intimidated by... you should be the woman that they want to have as a friend - a homegirl. I took that advice to heart. I've always been a girl's girl. Even now, when I'm at parties and events, I want to make sure that the women are taken care of and they're having a great time. My DMs and emails stay poppin' with women asking for advice, wanting to collaborate on charity events, and other things. I always answer those emails first, before any "you look beautiful" DM from any man. Creating that bond and sisterhood with other woman, especially on social media can be very beneficial and also good for the soul. It's like having an extended circle of family and friends, some that you'll never meet but they're just a click away. I'll always be thankful to KJ for instilling that in me.

April 2009 came around quickly; it was time to renew my contract because my original agreement was for two years only. I had just returned from New York where I was visiting a friend, feeling very refreshed with a whole new hustle and vibe glow. I guess that's what a few days in New York does to you. It makes you want to get out there and conquer the world. I usually went to work at 9:30 p.m. to prep for my 10:00 p.m. show but I had woken up to a call from KJ saying that he needed to see me around 2:00

p.m. Not thinking much of it, I got dressed and headed out to the radio station. Once I got there, I walked straight into KJ's office where he was sitting quietly answering emails on his laptop. He looked up at me and I could tell that it wasn't good. He even had tears in his eyes. Lord, what's about to happen? He told me to sit down and that he had some bad news. Clear Channel was doing a lot of cutbacks due to the recession and they were eliminating my show. Not because I wasn't good or had bad ratings, I actually had the best ratings at the radio station. Always number one and always making my bonuses. He told me that he had no choice but to eliminate whatever show was the latest in the day and obviously, that was the Quiet Storm. I stood there completely numb. There I was once again, getting my heart broken by my love, radio. Wow. He told me that I would receive severance pay for the next nine months but that I had to leave immediately. I didn't react. I wanted to cry but I couldn't. KJ was hurt, I could tell. He didn't want to let me go, especially since he knew how hard I worked to get here, but he had no choice. He walked me to my locker, so I could gather my things, and walked me out to the door. He gave me a big hug and said, "SunShyne, I will help you get a job somewhere else because you deserve to be on air. It may not be this year or the next, but I promise I will help you find something."

SunShyne was my radio name all throughout my radio career in Detroit. Back when I was an intern I was always so happy and cheerful whenever I came to work. I guess I was just excited to be there, so everyone there started to call me their little "sunshine". Later on, I started spelling it SunShyne to make it a bit special. But after a while, my friends started to call me Sunni for short and I got tired of going to the strip clubs and hearing "Sunshine is coming to the stage next" ... so I eventually became simply "Sunni".

Honestly, I couldn't quite say I believed KJ at that moment, but I nodded my head in agreement. I had a lump in my throat the size of a tennis ball and my tears were just holding on for dear life, trying not to fall. Overwhelmed with emotion, I walked away slowly carrying a few things from my locker, hoping I didn't collapse on the street. I got to my car and completely broke down, I must've sat there for an hour crying uncontrollably. What now? The highs and lows in my life were so extreme. Every time I reached a new high, I couldn't even fully enjoy it out of fear that it would all collapse to bring on a new low. I went to the nearest liquor store, got the biggest bottle of red wine I could find and went to Rian's house. We spent the evening drinking and crying. There was no plan B or

C, there were no plans at all. This was all I had, and it was gone. There I was, drunk, alone and unemployed. Again.

I've always been a "tough cookie" so to speak. Whenever I fell down, I gave myself three days to cry it out, punch the wall, whatever had to be done to get my frustration out, but then it was done. I would pick myself up and figure out what's next. Whenever I was by myself, I usually talked to myself in third person. It was a habit that came from always spending so much time in solitude. I asked myself, "What are we about to do next?" and went on from there. Being that I was getting my severance pay from WJLB for the next 9 months, I wasn't allowed to work at any other competing radio station. That was the clause in my contract. I did however get a weekend on air shift at our sister station Channel 955. It was a pop station and even though I loved pop music, I didn't think that my voice quite fit the station. But I took the job anyway and looked at it as another challenge. They weren't able to pay me for my time there because I was already collecting a check from Clear Channel, but I didn't mind because this gave me a chance to stay relevant on air, to improve my craft, work on my voice and get better.

It was about to be summer time so, I figured the best thing I could do was host parties and events to get some extra cash while I was still collecting my severance. Then I could save up to move. I always wanted to live in Miami. I had no idea what I wanted to do there but that was on my list of places to live. I was approaching my 26th birthday so I thought it would be the perfect time in my life to start something new. My only hesitation was the thought of leaving my family. I had to think about that many times over. We'd never been more than 30 minutes away from each other since we had moved to America from Bosnia. As much time as I had spent living on my own and chasing my dreams, I was never too far away to where I couldn't just hop in my car and go to a family dinner. My mother cooked every day, despite working long hours, that's just how she was. My dad loved her cooking and we never really ate out, even as teenagers. Sundays were special. My sister and her boyfriend, who would eventually become her husband, would come over and so would I, along with my laundry. It would be a big family day. My brother lived at my parent's house, so he would be there too. The relationship with my parents had gotten better over the years. We all had such strong personalities. We weren't very "mushy" so sometimes it seemed good for us to be apart and have our own space. But now I was planning to move a thousand miles away and they were concerned. I didn't have a plan for what I was going to do in Miami, but my time in Detroit has run its course. I needed a change of scenery. Radio had let me down so many times that I needed some time away from it, so if I had to waitress while I'm in Miami, I'd do it. I needed a fresh start. It was few days after my 26th birthday and I had just realized that my severance paycheck was ending that month. I had saved about five thousand dollars for my move and already booked my Miami apartment online. The plan was to sell everything that I had, pack up my little Nissan Altima and drive to Miami. But first I had to reassure my family that I was moving for a reason. I couldn't just tell them that I was moving to "find myself". They'd freak out and even worse, they'd constantly worry. I couldn't live with myself knowing that I was causing them any type of stress or grief. So, I made up this elaborate story about how I was moving there to work for a radio station, and how everything would be okay. In a way, I wasn't lying. I had already emailed a number of radio stations in Miami, but I hadn't heard anything back.

It was April 1st, , 2010, I packed everything I had into my Altima and headed for Miami. It was going to be a long trip and I was by myself. My first stop would be Atlanta where I planned to spend a night at my friend's house and finish the rest of my trip from there. For the first part of my trip, I drove in silence. No radio, no music, just me and my thoughts. I thought about what my plan was once I got to Miami, but my mind was drawing a blank. It was just me, I was the only human being I had to take care of and I'd been there before. No kids, no pets, no plants, just EYE had to stay alive. Even if I had to eat 4 chicken nuggets a day to survive off a dollar a day, I'd do it. Somewhere along the trip, I stopped to fill up my gas tank. It was a country town, maybe somewhere in Tennessee. I grabbed a honey bun from the gas station and sat in my car to eat it while my tank was filling up. While I was eating, I turned on my iPod and Drake's song, "Say What's Real" randomly came on. "Don't ever forget the moment you began to doubt, transitioning from fitting in to standing out" …those words struck me. Immediately, my heart started racing.

I felt like I was going to have a panic attack when I realized – I was terrified! I was moving thousands of miles away from the only family I had, with no job or plan. I was just chasing a dream that at moment, I didn't even know exists. But there I was, taking a leap of faith. I needed a new beginning. Not knowing my next move was as terrifying as it was exciting. But those words stayed with me. It was the moment I always look back on. Fear could've easily taken over and I could've turned around and went home. But I didn't. I turned up the radio, filled up my gas tank and prepared my mind for the adventure Miami would bring. Whatever would come, I was up for it.

THE SUNSHINE STATE

The breeze from the window hit my face as I opened the door to my beautiful Miami apartment. My apartment was right on Biscayne Ave overlooking downtown Miami and part of South Beach. It had been a long 24-hour drive from Michigan to Florida and I had just dragged my bags from the parking garage to the 18th floor. I was exhausted. Driving so many hours took a hard toll on my body that I ended up getting sick. I would spend the following two days recuperating. But once I got out of bed two days later, it was time to figure out my life. I woke up to an email from my friend, Necole Kane. Necole and I had worked together in the promotions department at WJLB in Detroit years before. She was there briefly and randomly disappeared, going to find her own "happiness". She now ran a very successful celebrity gossip blog called Necole Bitchie. From my Twitter, she had noticed that I had moved to Miami. To my surprise, she was living in Miami as well. After a few texts back and forth, we realized that we lived just five minutes from each other. Other than couple of DJs, I didn't know anyone else, so I was very happy to see a familiar face. We soon met up for dinner to catch up on old times. She told me how her blog kept her super busy and how successful it had become since the last time I saw her. I already knew because I use to check it religiously for my show prep when I hosted the Quiet Storm in Detroit. *"I think I'm going to leave radio alone for a while, it has just let me down too many time. I need to find a new career"*- I told her. Her knowing my history and how hard I worked to even be in this business, she said *"No, it's your calling. Take a short break, but not permanent"*. She then told me how hard it's been for her to manage the entire blog by herself and since I had no other employment lined up, she asked me to come work for her. YES! I have a job! My main focus working for Necole Bitchie site would be marketing and advertising. I also received an email from a program director of Power 96 in Miami who I had emailed a few weeks back. Apparently he knew about me from my Detroit days and was willing to offer me a Saturday afternoon shift.

Power 96 was a hip-hop/R&B/pop station with some Spanish flare, it was perfect for me. Things fell into place quickly. I always loved visiting Miami when I lived in Michigan. There was something about it, the people, the vibe, the weather... I was obsessed! But actually, living there turned out to be something completely different. It was so humid. And we're nothing talking about regular humidity, this was a "walk-outside-and-getcompletely-drenched" type of humidity. Especially if you were wearing business attire. FUEGO!! Necole and I worked a lot on the blog not leaving us much time to hit up the beach, plus it rained a lot that summer. By the time we'd finished up the blog stories, we'd eat dinner, chill and go to bed.

The next day, it was the same thing over and over. My Miami experience was definitely not turning out to be what I had expected. Dating wasn't that great either. Men in Miami approached women totally different than what I'd seen anywhere else. Maybe because it's such a tourist town and everyone is just passing by, having quick flings and moving on. I wanted more, I wanted to find and really date someone. So, when a guy named Cee asked me out to dinner, I thought okay, let's see where this goes. We had met earlier in the month as I was leaving Publix grocery story and he seemed like nice guy. Why not right? It was a beautiful evening as we met up to have sushi in the Brickell area of Miami. After chatting for a while about my life and how I was getting use to this Miami life, obviously I wanted to know more about him. He mentioned to me that he travels a lot from Miami to New York and I having friends on Wall Street that do the same assumed maybe he was in finance. When I asked him what he actually did for a living, he loudly said "I move dough, is that what you want me to say? Yea, I move weight from NYC to Miami, you're asking a lot for a first date." I just sat there with a blank stare on my face. We'd spent an hour talking about me but as soon as I wanted to know his occupation, it was asking too much? I was fed up, and I needed to find an exit quick. I excused myself to go to the restroom, snuck out the back door, and caught a cab back home. Thank God I didn't have him pick me up for the date like he had suggested because then he'd know where I live. I never saw him again anywhere after that. If this was how my dating life in Miami was going to go, I was already over it.

That summer in Miami was not at all what I had expected. Working for Power 96 on the weekends wasn't very fun. Big part of radio was getting to know the community and making a connection with the people that support you. I never got a chance to truly get into the community because I stayed busy with Necole Bitchie throughout the week. I also got a hostess job at Prime Italian to make a little extra money during the week. Every moment of the day I was exhausted. But from the outside looking in, you'd think I was living it up in Miami. That's how social media works. You paint the story you want others to see, not the actual reality of what it really is. After a long night at Prime Italian, I'd come home, post up in front of the television with some good food and catch up on all of my shows before heading out to stare at the computer all day for Necole Bitchie.com. That became my everyday life. Plus, I wasn't physically and mentally taking care of myself. I even gained fifteen pounds since my move and was falling back deep into my depression. I wondered if making this move to Miami was the right thing to do. I'd left my family behind in hopes of finding myself, but I felt like I was losing myself even more in the process. Reporting on celebrities had always been a part of my job in radio, but I had never been too caught up in that "entertainment life". I'd report on a story and keep it moving. It was hard working for a blog and having to write, create, and post stories daily about people living their glamorous lives all while I was struggling with my own. I hated it and Necole caught on to the fact I wasn't happy. I was also drinking heavy again and falling into my blackouts. It didn't take a lot for me to blackout and it was becoming way too normal for me, whether I drank a lot of not. I simply couldn't remember anything. One night as we hit the South Beach, nothing out of the ordinary, I just remember having a good time. Then bam, I feel the sun hitting my face. I open my eyes and realize that it's morning and that I'm sitting inside of my car. "Okay, I'm fine, I'm in once piece" I say to myself as I look around to see where I am and how I had gotten there. From what I can gather at the moment, I was sitting in my car with my windows down on Alton Street. Not sure what time I left the club, went to my friend's house, got my car from the building's valet and started driving home. Also, not quite clear at what point I decided that I was too lit to drive and pulled over to sleep on the side of the road WITH the windows down. Shocked that nobody robbed me, as my purse was open on the passenger seat, I gathered myself, closed my windows and proceeded to drive home. But I was still in such a daze from so much liquor that I felt like I was in a dream, driving, but not actually feeling my body pushing the gas or the breaks. I was floating. As I was making my way home, still in a daze, I can hear a woman's voice from a distance screaming at me in slow motion "Youuuuu're goinggggggggg the wronggggg wayyyyyyyyyyyyy"... It all felt like a nightmare I couldn't snap out of, I was going down the wrong way on the highway and there was a semi truck headed straight towards me. I finally snapped out of my drunkenness, swerved off the road and somehow managed to turn around. I made it home safely that morning, crawling into my bed slowly hoping to sleep off the demons of whatever happened the night before.

Earlier that summer, my sister shared that she and her husband were expecting their first son and I was so excited to get back home to see my family and celebrate. But I knew I would be bombarded with questions about Miami so I had to come up with an elaborate story about how amazing everything was and how I couldn't be happier. Again, I was lying to my family because I didn't want them to worry about me. No amount of pain that I'm in could be worse than seeing my family worry, because of me. Necole's blog was blowing up. She was getting exclusive celebrity interviews and photo-shoots so it wasn't long before she started talking about moving to New York City. It'd be great for the business and we'd be closer to all the celebrity action she said. Plus, since I wasn't happy in Miami, she suggested that I move too and we could work together out of New York. I thought about it for a day or two and said why not. Maybe I'll find something in New York that I've been missing in Miami. Here it is, just six months into my Florida experience and it was time to move again.

Necole left Miami at the end of October and I followed soon after. First I had to find someone to sell my furniture to and sublet my apartment. Thankfully, I knew a woman that worked closely with Young Money, Lil' Wayne's label. They needed a place to house their new artists so they took over my lease and I packed my things for New York City. I still had my car that I drove down from Detroit and driving it to NYC was not an option, especially since it was a lease and I couldn't afford to put all of those miles on it. So I packed everything I could fit into it and drove it to a train station in Orlando. The train would take me and the car up to Virginia. I had never taken the train before so the ride from Orlando to Virginia was pretty cool. I felt like I was in a time machine. I've never seen real train cars where they had real dining "rooms". Feeling anxious, I thought about skipping dinner because I didn't want to sit with strangers or worse, sit by myself and eat. As I relaxed in my unit, watching the trees zoom by, pretty sure we were somewhere in Georgia, I started seeing my whole life flash by me. What was I really going to do in New York? I had no real plan or desires. I hadn't planned to do radio since I hadn't reached out to any radio stations there. I also realized that working for the blog wouldn't last much longer because I wasn't happy and every day I hated it more and more. The voice in my head could be really encouraging or really self-doubting ... this time, it was both! "All these times, I kept getting knocked down but somehow I still found a way to get back up. Now that's impressive," I thought. But you aren't going all the way for it, Sunni!" My internal conversation continued. "You keep taking these leaps of faith, moving state to state but you're not truly taking the time to figure out what makes you truly happy. Yes, you have to work random jobs to get by but that doesn't mean that the other few hours of the day couldn't be spent working on yourself and your real goals and dreams."

"Wow, that's it," I thought, "stop, feeling bad for yourself and toughen up! You've come too far to get knocked back down, or worse, move back home, admitting that you really couldn't make this radio thing happen." Tears started falling down my face. I was alone and scared, but I knew God had my back. I picked up my makeup kit, fixed my face and decided to join the rest of the passengers for dinner in the dining cart. I ended up sitting next to the nicest older couple, who were probably able to tell that I was so lost in life. Quietly moving my food around, I kept my answers short as they tried to spark up a conversation. They could tell that I wasn't trying to be rude, just reserved. Then they started telling me stories of their families and many adventures that they had taken over the years. I started to envy them, they seemed so in love after all of these years, even holding hands as they continued the conversation well into the night. Before I headed back to my sleeping bunker, the lady turned to me and said "New York City is such a big place, what are you going to do there" ... I simply answered "I have no idea"

Nothing made me want to move to New York more than listening to Jay Z and Alicia Keys' song, Empire State of Mind. I remembered listening to that song in the summertime while still living in Detroit, imagining what it would be like to live in New York City. Every time I heard it, I daydreamed through every single lyric, hoping that one day I'd end up there. But I never expected it to be this soon and under these circumstances. As I walked out of the train station, the brisk fall air slapped me in the face. Winter was coming. It was going to be a long five-hour drive from Virginia to Brooklyn. Necole told me I could stay with her until I found my own place but being a guest in someone else's home had the expiration of dairy. So, I quickly started to look on Craigslist for an apartment. New York prices were way out of my budget and I was mentally preparing myself to accept the fact that I'd probably end up living in a bad neighborhood with bunch of roommates. I'm not the best person to live with, especially since I've never had a roommate or lived with anyone long term. My OCD kicks in, I vacuum at 8a.m. on the weekends, wash dishes at 3a.m. ... trust me, nobody wants to live with me.

I also came with the grips that I'd have to get rid of my car. That part I was not happy about - I loved driving! Maybe it was a Detroit thing, we are the Motor City and we didn't do a lot of public transportation. Omg how will I navigate through the NYC Subway system? I was panicking. After visiting a few people with possible rooms to rent, I quickly realized that living in New York City was not going to be an option for me. The apartments looked a tad bit better than what we had in the refugee camps. There were a bunch of people sharing rooms, pets were everywhere, and I could not handle it. Ew.

After searching for couple of weeks, I found a pretty good listing from a woman named Robin, but she lived across the river in Jersey. She was willing to rent me small room on the second floor of her house, where her and her husband's master bedroom was also located, with their kids' room directly across from mine for $600 per month. Also, I was going to be able to use her kitchen and laundry room as I please AND there was plenty of parking on the street for my car. This was perfect! I didn't plan on having visitors over (especially not men) so I didn't mind sharing a space with family since they were out during most of the day anyway. Robin turned out to be my guarding angel in disguise. She was so welcoming to me and treated me as if I was a part of the family. Thanksgiving break was coming up and I had made plans to go back to Michigan to visit my family. I'd only been in New York for a month, but things weren't quite going the way I had planned. One morning I woke up and wrote a long email to Necole basically telling her that I would like to quit working for her and the blog. She has always been very good to me, but the constant celebrity obsession that comes with working for a blog had finally reached its peak for me. In radio, reporting on celebrities had never been a problem for me because after I left my show, I never thought about it again. I still got to do all the things I loved without having to constantly stay on top of all the latest breaking celebrity news as I did with the blog. I had enough and I'm pretty sure Necole saw it coming because she knew for a while that I wasn't happy. I reassured her that it wasn't personal and that I needed to figure out what the next steps in my life will be. She responded to my email quickly with some encouraging words and well wishes, and it was over. So, there I was in New York City where dreams come true, unemployed.

BIG CITY, NOT SO BRIGHT LIGHTS

It was the day before I was to fly back home for Thanksgiving to spend the week with my family. I had booked my plane ticket a while back while I was still making money but now, I found myself with no money and no other income coming in. Rent was almost due and Necole had just paid me my last paycheck, so I needed to figure out something quickly. I got dressed in my best professional attire, which wasn't much, slacks and an old tired button-down shirt. That year, I had spent so much time working and moving around, I wasn't left with much time or money for new wardrobe. I kept a lot of my summer clothes from Miami and would layer them with some key pieces to make an outfit. There was no room left in my budget for any extra spending, so I used what I had to make it work. I drove into the city and left my car on the upper West side. By now I had figured out my way around the city and always found free parking depending on the day. My Detroit friend Alexis was working for a financial firm and told me to swing by and have lunch with her. I thought this would be a perfect time to inquire about a receptionist's position at her company, so I happily accepted the offer. The city was pretty cold and damp that day and I decided to walk the 30 blocks from my car to her building. I wanted to explore the neighborhood a bit and didn't want to spend any extra money on cabs. Thank God I had worn flats because thirty blocks in heels would've been hell. As I walked aimlessly through the streets, checking out a few stores along the way, knowing I couldn't afford anything, I received a text from Alexis telling me that she had to postpone lunch to another day because something came up. Shit! Did I just waste $8 that I had to pay at the tolls to come into New York from Jersey? That was my biggest issue living in New Jersey, deciding whether crossing into New York would be worth the $8 I'd have to pay at the toll. With not much else planned for the day, and not much money to spend on anything in the city, I decided to treat myself to a glass of wine at a nearby restaurant. It was between a cab ride back to the car or the wine. I chose the wine. There was a small neighborhood restaurant on 3rd street called Le Bistro Steak and at the time it looked pretty empty, so I decided to go in and have my wine at the bar while the rain passed. The atmosphere was pretty nice inside and the bartender and I quickly became friends. After chatting for a few minutes, and me partially telling him my entire life story, he tells me that the owner of the restaurant is also Yugoslavian and waives him over to us. His name was Nick and he looked a lot like the men in my family, that Yugoslavian face, the strong face features and the strong accent. He asked me what I was doing in New York and we struck up a friendly conversation. I told him that I was scared to go back home tomorrow knowing that I'm jobless and today didn't pan out the way I expected as I was gunning for a receptionist's position a few blocks over. He immediately said, "why don't you come work for me, have you ever been a hostess before?". I told him that I was a hostess for a brief time in Miami at Prime Italian and he immediately said, "You're hired; can you start after Thanksgiving break?" Wow. What a blessing! I was so relieved. The stress of not knowing where my next paycheck was going to come from was finally lifted off my shoulders and I could enjoy time with my family without worry. Nick told me that he'd pay me hourly plus I could make tips as a hostess by checking people's coats in. He informed me that he has some VIP clients and that they would always tip well if I took their coats or seated them fast. Even the Mayor of New York was a regular there.

The trip home was a much-needed break for me. I needed some family love and laughter. It was a crazy year for me and I just wanted to sit still for a moment and enjoy some good Bosnian food and family time. My nephew, Liam, was born just couple of weeks before Thanksgiving and it was my first time seeing him. He was so beautiful, and I immediately fell in love with him. Seeing my sister's family grow and blossom just reminded me of how much of a personal life I didn't have. I was focusing so much on trying to figure out my career path, I had completely abandoned my love life. But I had decided to sign up for Match.com earlier that week so I was looking forward to my upcoming dates. Turns out, dating in New York isn't as easy as they make it seem on Sex and The City. My first date on Match.com was a cop that ended up being super weird and would not stop calling me. Super creeper!! The next guy was pretty good looking and worked on Wall Street, but after the first date, I immediately realized that he may be on the down low. He gave me a vibe like he was "trying" to date women to maybe prove that he wasn't gay. I loved my gay guy friends and I had plenty of them, so spotting someone on the low wasn't very hard. Clearly, Match .com was not working for me, so I quickly ended up deleting my account.

I couldn't tell my family that I wasn't working with Necole anymore or that I was about to be a hostess at a restaurant, remember, they're very judgy. So, I made up this elaborate story how I'm doing on-air reports for Hot 97 just to make them think that I was progressing in my career. In actuality, I did do couple of celebrity reports for Necole Bitchie on Hot 97 but it was nothing major and it was only for one week. Not having any other leads or plans, I returned back to New York and started working as a hostess right after the Thanksgiving break. My work hours were 5pm until 11pm, 6 days a week. That left me plenty of time during the day to sleep in, research things online and figure out what my next step would be. I even started writing a personal blog to keep my Twitter followers informed on my NYC adventures. Wendy Williams had just launched a TV show and I was addicted! Not having to search for stories and gossip every minute of the day made me feel free, so catching up on the latest gossip felt good once in a while. I wasn't really sure if I was ready to jump into radio again, so I didn't reach out to any Program Directors in the area. Necole had always told me that I'd get back in radio at some point, but I would usually just brush it off. For now, I decided to just sit still for a minute, work my little hostess job and save some money.

The money I was making was enough to pay my rent and to get back and forth from Jersey to New York.

Not leaving me much money for anything extra. Robin, my house host, would help me out by buying some of my favorite foods when she went to the store as if I was her own kid. She'd also let me use her hair products and would even buy extra body washes and feminine products if I needed them. She truly saved me, as I had legit been living paycheck to paycheck, depending on any extra tips I made by checking coats and playing "the sweet hostess". Most of my time, outside of work, was spent on the Jersey side. I felt more comfortable being somewhere where I could drive around, pull up and park right in front of a store. The suburbia felt more like home.

It was a cold December day and the Christmas shopping season was in full effect. My family and I don't celebrate Christmas so I didn't have to worry about buying anyone any gifts, not that I was able to afford them anyway. I really wanted to buy myself a windbreaker jacket so I could go jogging around the neighborhood. By now, I had let myself go and gained a few pounds and getting a gym membership was not in my price range. I had about $50 in my bank account so I figured TJ Maxx was a good place to stop by hoping to find a nice jacket on clearance. As I strolled through a TJ Maxx, I received a call from a 301-area code. Since I didn't know anyone with that number, I declined the call and kept shopping. They didn't leave a message so I assumed that they dialed the wrong number. The same call came in the next day and the day after. I finally answered. It was Michael Sanders, a big-time Program Director that worked for CBS Radio. He used to be a Program Director at my old radio station in Detroit, WJLB, but that was way back before I even started working with them years prior. He asked me what I was doing in New York and I was speechless because first, "how did he know I was in New York" and secondly, "how did Michael even know who I was?" We chatted briefly about my stint on-air in Miami but he was very vague, not giving me a clear reason for his call. After he hung up, I didn't think much of his call. Maybe he'll keep me in mind for some future on-air opportunities I thought. A week went by and I received another call, this time was from Atlanta. Reggie Rouse, the Vice President of Urban Programming for CBS was calling me and again, I was in shock.

"Why were these people calling me and how did they even know who I was?" I thought. They weren't giving me many answers. My first thought when Reggie called me from Atlanta was "OMG, he's going to offer me a job in Atlanta," then that excitement quickly turned into "OMG, there aren't many straight men in Atlanta, I'm never going to get married".

Well, it wasn't Atlanta. It was Washington D.C. What? Washington D.C.? I'd only been there once when Necole and I flew in to cover Wale and Kevin Durant's charity weekend earlier that year. It was a beautiful place but I didn't know much about it, outside of the clubs and restaurants we had visited that weekend. My friend Monique had moved there a year prior and now she was living with her boyfriend, who soon after became her husband. She was the only person I knew in DC. Reggie told me that there may be an on-air spot opening soon and that he'd like for me to come in and interview for it. I happily accepted without getting any other clear details about the on-air position. The big Snowmaggedon storm was coming and it was predicted to hit the East coast HARD the week of my interview. No way that was going to stop me from getting to DC and impressing these people, I thought. I woke up early the day of my interview and mapped out my route to DC to be sure to avoid tolls, I had no extra money other than to cover the gas for the trip so I figured taking the long way was my best and only option. The snow had just started to fall, it was 3am as I got into my Nissan Rogue, said my prayers and headed to Washington DC. I had no clue which station or which shift they were looking for, it was a job interview and I just knew that I had to be there at 10am. After 6 hours driving through the back roads of God knows where, I finally made it to DC thirty minutes before my interview. I had stopped along the way at a gas station and changed from my sweatpants into a more appropriate interview outfit, a black dress and black tights. It was my go-to outfit, especially in New York. I wasn't buying extra clothes so that outfit had gotten recycled so many times, I just switched up the jewelry. During my interview process, I learned that a year prior, KJ Holiday, my old Program Director from Detroit, had sent my demo air-check out to all of the PDs hoping to find me a job. Since there were no openings at the time, they kept it on file and called me now, a year later. I was stunned. KJ had been my mentor and I knew how hard it was for him to fire me from WJLB. He promised me that he would help me get a job eventually. He said, "it may not be this year or the next, but one day." And he kept his promise. He was such an incredible man. Our schedules were always conflicting when I was in town to visit family so I never got to truly thank him in person for everything that he did for me. A few years later I learned that he had a heart attack while playing basketball with his son and died. It was heartbreaking to hear, he was only in his 50s.

The interview went well and afterwards I drove straight back to New York. I didn't know if I had gotten the job or not, but I didn't let that distract me from going to work and pressing on with life. It was New Year's Eve 2010 going into 2011. My restaurant boss Nick told me that he'd let me get off work a little earlier so that I could meet my friends at a nearby club to ring in the New Year. By this time, I had made some friends along the way, but also kept in close touch with my Detroit friends. I told myself that life in New York was a passing phase and that I wouldn't be there long. On our way to the club, all the girls crammed in a cab, one of the girls revealed to us that she had breast cancer. She wasn't my closest friend, but I knew her through one of the other girls. Once inside the bar, we got situated with some of their other friends and decided to forget about everything that had just happened and have a great time. While standing on a couch, I saw a commotion between some of my friends and the people at the table next to us. All of a sudden, I saw a random girl swing a punch and hit our friend right in the face, the one that had just told us she had cancer. The next few minutes weren't very clear because I completely blacked out. I felt my body lift off the ground as I flew across the table and started to punch the girl that initiated the commotion. The rage in me was indescribable. Most of it obviously was because I was trying to defend my friend, but I couldn't help but feel that also it came from another place. I'd been hurting for a while and this was the perfect time for me to let it out. Take it out on somebody. It was as if someone put me in a room and said go crazy, so I did. I went off on this girl so hard that it took multiple security guards to rip us apart. I had big rings on my fingers and my right hook is pretty nice. I felt like I was a boxer who didn't hear the bell ring.... I just kept going. Because the girl and her friends initiated the fight, they were kicked out of the bar and we were allowed to stay and celebrate. What a way to bring in the New Year... a pretty crazy end to a wild year.

Driving back and forth to New Jersey was becoming too much for me as I was trying to cut back the cost of living, so I decided that it would be cheaper if I live in my car for a bit in the city. The plan was that I'd work evenings at the restaurant until 11p.m., sleep in my car overnight (which I'd park for free on the Upper West side), go to the local gym in the morning since cost of the gym membership is better than rent, use their showers, and spend the rest of the day job hunting or just exploring the city. I hadn't heard back about the radio job in D.C., so I started to make new plans on how to survive New York until something big came along. The plan sounded pretty good until I read how a man died while sleeping in his car because he left it running and the carbon monoxide killed him. It was still cold out, so I knew that I'd have to leave my car ON while I slept, so now it looks like this plan was a no go.

I continued to work at the restaurant and keep my spirits up all while waiting patiently on a call from D.C. I needed to know if I had gotten to the job or not, the suspense was killing me. It was January of 2011 and my phone rang, 301 area code, I had gotten the job! I couldn't wait to tell Nick at the restaurant that I was quitting soon and getting back on the radio. I told fabulous stories of my life back in Detroit when I was working on-air to Nick and everyone who would listen at the restaurant. They probably felt like saying, "Girl, go seat those people at table 5" but I was excited! Finally, my dream position, middays 10am to 2p.m., which I've always wanted to do since the days when I was an intern for Kris Kelley. The station was WPGC 95.5, which I didn't know much about, but I had heard that it was a heritage station similar to WJLB in Detroit, so I knew that I'd fit in just fine. For the next month, I'd drive to D.C. on the weekends to do on-air shifts and get familiar with the studio equipment.

Money was tight since I was taking time away from the restaurant to drive all the way to D.C., but I technically wasn't making any money in D.C. yet. Robin agreed to let me pay my rent in two separate parts since I was going to be moving out soon. She was very sad to see me go, but knowing my whole backstory, she was very excited for this new chapter of my life.

Soon, it was time to move again. I packed my entire life into my Nissan Rogue and drove to D.C. to do one last weekend shift on-air. In two weeks, I was to start full time on –air doing my midday position 10a.m. to 2p.m. It felt so good to be back on! Because radio had kicked my ass over the years, I had almost given up on it but being back on in a big city felt sooo right. After my shift, I drove from D.C. to Detroit to spend some quality time with my family for a week before I start my new gig. My family was pretty excited that I was going to be on-air in D.C. I had to make it sound extra grand to them because I wanted them to be as excited about it as I was. Funny, because Necole kept telling me that she knew I'd get back to radio one day and I always doubted her. Now it was all coming full circle. In ten months, I'd gone from Detroit to Miami to New York to D.C. I'd spent endless sleepless nights full of tears, fears and uncertainty but finally, there I was again. Back on the radio!

After spending a much-needed week with my family, I drove back to D.C. to start my new exciting job as a midday host on the legendary WPGC 95.5. I drove back alone, as usual, spending most of the drive in silence, caught up in my thoughts. I couldn't help but think back about a year ago, when I drove from Detroit to Miami. Man, I was terrified. I had no job lined up, no friends, no leads and no goals. Taking that leap of faith changed my life. Everything that came after was a test: having to work multiple jobs, lying to my family, feeling depressed and emotionally drained most of the time, it all had to happen for this moment here. Thankfully, KJ sent out my air-check hoping someone would have an opening and give me chance. Wow. I could've easily blasted WJLB on social media after they let me go. I could've easily retweeted all the people that were cursing them out asking why I wasn't doing the Quiet Storm anymore. But I didn't. I learned that in business you must keep it professional at all times. Other stations could've seen me as wild and not worth the headache if I had publicly bashed my previous employer. But I didn't. I looked at everything as a challenge and a lesson. And here I am, thinking back to the day when I heard the words to that song and how it echoed in my soul… "Don't ever forget the moment you began to doubt, transitioning from fitting in to standing out" … Here I am, vividly remembering that moment. Thanking God for the journey.

After so much time of feeling like a butterfly, going where the wind took me, it was all starting to make sense. Things were finally coming together. The little girl from Bosnia who overcame hunger, poverty, fear … had proven herself and remained strong through it all, in America. There were times I felt alone, hungry, cold, depressed and worse – yet, I fought through it. I found the strength within. But moving to D.C. was terrifying at the same time. Will they like me there? Will they turn on the radio and say who is this girl? I only had one friend there so … who will I hang out with? What if my ratings are terrible and nobody tunes in? No, you can't think that way

Sunni. What if it all works out? What if you're welcomed with opened arms in this amazing city? What if your ratings skyrocket and you become the star of your station? What if you meet many beautiful people who end up being your friends for life? What if you become this amazing philanthropist who ends up helping many who are in the same spot that you use to be in? What if you settle in and buy a house in D.C., get into a happy healthy relationship and live happily ever after? What if? ... You change every single terrifying thought into a great optimistic one ...

I try to live life with no regrets and that can be hard. It feels good to say that, but how many of us actually have no regrets? Instead of calling them regrets, let's call them lessons. Everything we do in life is a lesson. It teaches us, it strengthens us, it makes us reevaluate the next move. One of my biggest "lessons" in life was never finishing college. Not being a college graduate made me feel small in a room full of educated D.C., folks whenever I attended a party or a fancy happy hour. Because in D.C., it's all about what school you went to and what job you have. My personality is so big, loud, and fun ... but that was the one thing that would make me retrieve back to my insecurities and not feel worthy enough. It made me feel like I'm just some tatted up, loud radio girl who probably shouldn't be in this room. When asked what year I graduated, I'd usually say 2006 (because that would've been my year if I had finished) or I'd quietly say that I left right before graduation to pursue my career. To see someone like me who is usually so confident and outgoing experience such anxiety when asked those questions is a sight to see. But I couldn't help but feel that way.

So, I started looking at it this way...

There are so many people in the world who went on to do amazing things in life without finishing school. They went on to build companies, create wealth, and help others. I had to stop measuring myself up to others based on their credentials. Once I learned to see everyone for who they really are, how they got to where they were at, and all the hard work they put in, it started to inspire me and uplift me. Now, I was admiring them because of their hard work, dedication, sacrifice and passion. It wasn't about the degrees and awards. It was about what they had done for the world or how they helped the people around them. In my mind, I started stripping people of all their fancy shit and seeing them as humans, who just happened to have a fabulous job that allows them to be rich. That's how I started seeing everyone. There will always be people who are richer than you, smarter than you and have more degrees than you. If you're constantly comparing your worth based on others' achievements, you will never win.

In the words of Kendrick Lamar, BE HUMBLE. Appreciate every single thing you earned and be proud of it – celebrate it! Never feel like you aren't good enough AT THIS very moment just because you haven't gotten to your destination yet. Life is truly a journey and along the way we collect experiences, people, and memories. It's supposed to be hard, but it can also be beautiful if you let it be. I always say that I'm just a regular girl who just happened to have a fabulous job that allows me to connect with and help the world, whether in a big way or small.

My beautiful journey showed me that through times, light or darkness, the power that I've always had within myself would prevail. I also realize now more than ever, how having my family there made a difference in the best of times and the worst of times. Weather we agreed or not, they were exactly what I needed to push myself to greatness. Them being skeptical and critical of my decisions wasn't because of some selfish reasons, it was because they were scared for my future. That's what parents do. But my belief in myself had to be bigger than my parents' fear for me.

If everything was taken away from me tomorrow, I know I have the confidence to lace up my big girl boots, get back out there and figure out what's next. That's the beauty of life. Change is the only constant thing.

CPSIA information can be obtained
at www.ICGtesting.com
Printed in the USA
BVHW051558220119
538364BV00012B/399/P